P9-CEF-582

The Bel-Air

BOOK OF SOUTHERN CALIFORNIA
FOOD AND ENTERTAINING

THE Bel-Air

BOOK OF SOUTHERN CALIFORNIA
FOOD AND ENTERTAINING

NORMAN KOLPAS
WITH
GEORGE MAHAFFEY,
EXECUTIVE CHEF OF THE HOTEL BEL~AIR

PHOTOGRAPHY BY BRIAN LEATART

CROWN PUBLISHERS, INC.
NEW YORK

THE BEL-AIR BOOK OF SOUTHERN CALIFORNIA FOOD AND ENTERTAINING was prepared and produced by
Kenan Books, Inc. 15 West 26th Street, New York, New York 10010

Editor: Sharon Kalman
Designer: Robert W. Kosturko
Photography Editor: Christopher Bain
Production Director: Karen L. Greenberg

Copyright © 1991 by Kenan Books, Inc.

Photographs copyright © by Brian Leatart

All rights reserved. No part of this book may be reproduced or transmitted in any form or by any means, electronic or
mechanical, including photocopying, recording, or by any information storage and retrieval system, without permission in
writing from the publisher.

Published by Crown Publishers, Inc., 201 East 50th Street, New York, New York 10022. Member of the Crown
Publishing Group.

CROWN is a trademark of Crown Publishers, Inc.

Printed and bound in Italy by Eurograph spa

Library of Congress Cataloging-in-Publication Data

Kolpas, Norman.
The Bel-Air Book of Southern California Food and Entertaining / by
Norman Kolpas w/ George Mahaffey.
p. cm.
Includes index.
1. Cookery, American—California style. 2. Hotel Bel-Air (Los
Angeles, Calif.) 3. Entertaining. I. Title.
TX715.2.C34K65 1991
641.59794—dc20
                                        91-8746
                                        CIP

ISBN 0-517-58414-X

10 9 8 7 6 5 4 3 2 1

First Edition

DEDICATION

*To the memories of Alphonzo Bell and Joseph Drown,
whose visions continue to be realized daily at Hotel Bel-Air.*

And to Caroline Rose Hunt.

ACKNOWLEDGMENTS

Many dedicated friends and colleagues of the authors and photographer contributed their time, expertise, and insight in the development of this book. Special thanks go to the current and former staff members of Hotel Bel-Air; Norman Stewart, food stylist; Tom Kaufman, sommelier at Hotel Bel-Air; Al Peiler, head gardener at Hotel Bel-Air; Mona Devich and Clifford Miller, flower stylists; Christofle, Beverly Hills, for providing exquisite china, silver, and crystal featured in the photographs; and Tesoro, Beverly Hills, for the use of select tableware for photography.

INTRODUCTION

SOUTHERN CALIFORNIA FOOD AND ENTERTAINING

IN ITS RARE COMBINATION OF NATURAL BLESSINGS, EASYGOING STYLE, and honest-to-goodness substance, Southern California epitomizes the good life.

The weather alone draws a steady stream of visitors and settlers. Add to that an ever-changing panorama of beautiful scenery—snowcapped mountains and gentle foothills, the Pacific coastline, and the austere inland deserts—and you have, in climate and geography alone, a recipe for paradise.

No doubt an awareness of the region's perfection contributed to a tone of casual, easy living here from the time the earliest Spanish settlers arrived just over two centuries ago. Southern California offered then, as it does now, a sense of limitless opportunity, coupled with unparalleled abundance and unbridled hospitality. As nineteenth-century California historian Hubert Howe Bancroft wrote of the region's early days, "a person could travel from San Diego to Sonoma without a coin in his pocket, and never want for a roof to cover him, a bed to sleep on, food to eat, and even tobacco to smoke."

From the early idyllic rancho estates to the rush of health seekers sent here by their doctors in the latter part of the nineteenth century, Southern California came to typify a lifestyle of openness and well-being. With the growth of the motion-picture industry, glamour was added to the list of glowing adjectives. And today, it stands on the brink of even greater achievement as America's commercial and cultural doorway to the Pacific Rim.

Throughout its relatively brief history, Southern California has, not surprisingly, evolved its own unique style of cooking and entertaining—a style that has come vibrantly into its own since the late 1970s, when the late great Jean Bertranou of l'Ermitage in Los Angeles first applied his expert knowledge of classic and nouvelle French cuisine to the region's abundant produce and casual lifestyle. Since that time, a distinctive local approach to food and its enjoyment has evolved to the point that many experts now consider Southern California the nation's most exciting culinary region.

But what precisely *is* the Southern California dining experience? That question gets asked emphatically and repeatedly because the very same reasons that make the cuisine unique and exciting—its openness, its eclecticism, and its celebration of a dizzyingly wide gamut of fresh ingredients—also make it somewhat difficult to precisely define.

When it comes to cooking and dining, the relaxed nature of the Southern California lifestyle translates to an openness to the many different cultural and ethnic influences alive in the region. "People here have a fairly high culinary IQ," says the Hotel Bel-Air's executive chef George Mahaffey, using a term he has coined to express not just a knowledge of food, but also an intelligent willingness to try new things. An avid dining public cannot help but inspire restaurateurs and chefs to ever higher heights of culinary creativity, which often involves combining different elements from European, Asian, African, or Latin American cooking in the same dish or on the same menu—adding tropical

fruits, for example, to a classic crème brulée, or elaborating a teatime menu with crisp little Chinese spring rolls.

And just as superb materials can spur on an artist, so do the fresh ingredients available in Southern California excite the region's cooks and define another aspect of their cuisine. "The aim," says Mahaffey, "is to use fresh produce as much as possible." And that's not just supermarket-fresh, as opposed to canned or frozen. "I'm talking more in terms of vine- or tree-ripened products, relying on small producers to give us a really nice strawberry, or a great peach, or a different variety of very flavorful tomato." With its benevolent climate and fertile soil, Southern California meets those demands, encouraging an ever-growing

number of small-scale farmers and gardeners, who excite cooks with everything from just-picked herbs to all kinds of flavorful, colorful, and intricately shaped baby salad leaves; from cultivated chanterelles and other once-rare mushrooms to bell peppers in a rainbow of different hues. Fishermen, cattlemen, poultry ranchers, and other food producers respond overwhelmingly to Southern California's desire for quality and variety. Happily, it's a trend one can find evidence of in markets across the country.

Truly fresh vegetables and fruits, poultry, meats, and seafood have extraordinarily vivid flavor, and Southern California cuisine strives to emphasize that fresh taste. That's why brief cooking is such a hallmark here—most evident in the penchant for grilling, a cooking method also wonderfully well suited to outdoor living.

The emphasis on freshness shows, too, in the way foods are seasoned and sauced. While classic European-style cooking often aims to concoct intricate mélanges of flavor, for the most part Southern California dishes present ingredients fairly simply. Herbs and spices are carefully selected to emphasize an ingredient's natural taste; brief smoking over aromatic woods is sometimes used to add extra flavor to everything from the obvious choice of meats to less obvious candidates like cheese, vegetables, and even fruits.

For the same reason, heavy or rich sauces are almost nonexistent— replaced instead by light dressings, vegetable purees, freshly chopped salsas, or fruit essences that show off the dish's flavor in a bold new light. Grilled seafood, for example, shuns the beurre blanc that might have been served with it a decade or more ago, in favor of, say, a balsamic vinaigrette or a chunky salsa of tomatoes and chiles. In place of the demiglace that might once have sauced a roasted pheasant, the rich, sweet meat may now find a more natural companion in a light fruit essence.

In presentation, too, the emphasis on freshness remains supreme. "You want sparkling freshness in the way food looks," says Mahaffey, "and our style of cooking shows a meticulous desire for fresh colors and textures to match the flavors." While there is no one particular Southern California way to place food on a plate, presentations—though certainly artful— lack the overworked fussiness one often sees in more classic cooking.

And, like the lifestyle itself, all the trappings of serving a meal in Southern California lean toward the casual. Even the most formal occasions are refreshingly free of stuffiness or pretense. Since the climate makes such a vital contribution to that easygoing style, hosts and hostesses take full advantage of the weather and the setting when possible—holding parties in the garden or on the patio, or at the very least in a location with a view of the outdoors.

Wherever you go, you'll find examples of this appealing approach to entertaining—in posh restaurants and casual bistros, public parks and private homes. But ask anyone who truly knows Southern California to name one place that exemplifies the region and its lifestyle, and chances are they'll point you in the direction of the Hotel Bel-Air.

Left: *Executive chef George Mahaffey and his staff use the freshest ingredients available; something the home chef can easily do, too.*
Right: *Pan-Roasted Peppered Baby Lamb Chop and Minipotato Gallette with Balsamic Vinaigrette (recipe on page 109).*

Ask them why the Bel-Air merits such a distinction, and you're likely to hear the same few comments over and over again. They'll talk about its seclusion, its calm serenity, its quiet glamour. They'll mention the beauty of the Spanish-influenced architecture, with its pink-stucco walls and red-tile roofs. They'll laud the impeccable yet friendly service, and, of course, the outstandingly fresh, always surprising cuisine.

They'll remark that when you leave your car and cross the covered footbridge—which spans the sunken front gardens and offers a view of the Bel-Air's signature swans floating tranquilly on their lake—you are overcome with the feeling that you've entered a different world.

In looks and in spirit, the Hotel Bel-Air is very much a place *of* Southern California. Having grown with one of Los Angeles' most prestigious and secluded communities, the hotel reflects, in microcosm, everything that is idyllic about living here: the sunshine, the relaxation, the glamour, the abundance of pleasures. Tucked well away beyond Bel-Air's open gates, and nestled between Stone Canyon's steep hillsides, the hotel also remains untouched by all that one might think of as drawbacks to modern Los Angeles: the traffic, the tourists, the billboards, the deal making. Summer temperatures are markedly cooler here, winter chills slightly less chilling. The canopy of leaves that shelters the hotel seems to filter out the world.

In a real yet rare way, the Hotel Bel-Air distills the timeless essence of Southern California. And this book, in turn, aims to explore the very best of Southern California food and entertaining by distilling, in words, recipes, and images, the essence of the Hotel Bel-Air: the charm of its architecture and interiors, the lush serenity of its gardens, and most of all, the casual yet stylish pleasure of dining here.

The menus and recipes on the following pages have been conceived and selected not only because they represent the full gamut of Southern California food and entertaining as captured by the Hotel Bel-Air dining experience, but also because they are readily applicable to the home kitchen and to the many ways in which we all entertain. Browse through them; adapt menus to suit your needs and tastes; try individual recipes that appeal to you. Let this book be as comfortably accommodating to you as the Bel-Air kitchen is to any guest who stays or dines at the hotel—and, indeed, as Southern California has always been to anyone who has visited or settled in this blessed part of the world.

HOTEL BEL-AIR: A BRIEF HISTORY

A mid-1930s real estate brochure entitled "Bel-Air: Aristocrat of Residential Parks" included a full-page photograph of two genteel, formally dressed ladies sitting outdoors on redwood lawn furniture, sipping tea from china cups beneath the lofty branch of a sycamore tree from which a single, bare light bulb is suspended. In the background, beside a rustic building half-hidden by foliage, a sign reads "Bel-Air Tea Room."

It's a charming image that perfectly presages the great hotel that would begin life on that very site some ten years later. Today, the building that housed the tearoom—also known by the name "The Sycamores"—is the hotel's lobby. The unique combination of elegance and casualness captured in the photo still holds sway in every aspect of the hotel's lifestyle.

Alphonzo Bell would have approved. At the beginning of the 1920s, Bell, a gentleman farmer who struck oil on his land in Rancho Santa Fe, near San Diego, purchased a vast tract of Los Angeles hillside just west of Beverly Hills. There, in 1922, he began to develop what he envisioned as the premiere Southern California residential park. And a name for it came conveniently to mind: In the region's Spanish days, the parcel had been called Rancho San José de Buenos Aires; Bell threw in a variation on his own surname, and changing the Spanish, he arrived at "Bel-Air."

As he subdivided the steep canyons and gently rolling vales of Bel-Air into housing sites, Bell lavished improvements everywhere. The Bel-Air Country Club was incorporated into the overall plan. Landscape experts labored to supplement the native sycamores, California live oaks, and other sparse but hearty vegetation common to the semiarid climate, resulting in a gladelike setting for the custom work of the era's leading residential architects.

The heart of the community was, logically enough, Bell's arcaded, mission-style real estate office and administration building on Stone Canyon Road. Here, a bridle trail began, winding its way throughout Bel-Air, enhancing the aura of true country living. North of the office, Bell constructed a stable where local residents could board their horses, and a riding ring where equestrians could polish and display their horsemanship. As Bell's offices became more of a gathering point, the tearoom—which also served luncheons and dinners—naturally followed.

This courtyard was added to the hotel in 1982, yet one would never know that it was not a part of the original hotel.

By the early 1940s, Bel-Air was well along its way towards fulfilling Bell's vision, and there seemed less and less need for its founder to maintain his offices. There was talk of allowing a multiple-story hotel to be built on the site, but that would not have been in keeping with the community's low profile.

Finally, Bell met a man with a vision to match his own: Joseph Drown, a Texas hotelier who had fallen in love with Southern California. "I wanted to create a model of what the first-time visitor to California should experience in our state," said Drown, explaining the hotel he dreamed of creating. He commissioned prominent architect Burton Schutt to adapt and extend the existing one- and two-story buildings into "a relatively small, typically California structure, built around gardens and patios, an indoor/outdoor world with the feeling of a very private place."

Offices and stables became bungalow-style guest rooms, some with private patios, some with fireplaces. More rooms were added in a similar spirit, bringing the total to sixty-two, with no two rooms alike in size or shape.

Everywhere, Drown directed teams of gardeners in the creation of an informal Eden, filled with bougainvillea, pink-blossomed floss silk trees, ferns, palms, roses, camellias, azaleas, peaches, apricots, figs, and redwoods, complete with a Swan Lake fed by waters from the Stone Canyon Reservoir. Like so many other things in Southern California, few of the plants were native: They planted big tipuana trees from Bolivia, stately Arizona cypresses, delicate Japanese maples, and Australian tree ferns. Yet, over the years, these superb specimens have combined readily with native vegetation to form a subtropical paradise. And, while the plants are impeccably tended to and cared for, they are not meticulously manicured like the plants in a formal, European-style garden. Nature, after all, is never quite perfect.

The Hotel Bel-Air welcomed its first guests in 1946, and it swiftly established a reputation as the ultimate Southern California retreat-within-the-city. Not surprisingly, it became a favorite with Hollywood celebrities—with one fine distinction: Those luminaries who wished to be seen, who sought publicity, stayed a few miles away at the Beverly Hills Hotel, but those who desired privacy, those whom other stars and studio dignitaries came to see, tucked themselves away at the Bel-Air. They particularly prized the fact that they could reach their rooms

Opposite page: *Overlooking Swan Lake, The Terrace is a beautiful, tranquil place to relax and enjoy the food at the Hotel Bel-Air.* **Above:** *When you enter the Hotel Bel-Air, your are instantly transported into a different world.*

The lush landscaping and private corners of the Hotel Bel-Air were favored by such Hollywood stars as Grace Kelly, Marilyn Monroe, and Laurence Olivier.

through the hotel's numerous private gates and sheltered pathways, without passing through the lobby.

The Bel-Air zealously guarded their privacy, and it continues to do so: Only the names of Hollywood legends now deceased are normally mentioned by hotel staff. Young Grace Kelly was a regular, long-staying guest when she was filming in Hollywood. Soon after her marriage, Princess Grace of Monaco brought her husband Prince Rainier back to the hotel specifically to introduce him, shyly, to waiters and maids, bell-boys and managers, whom she had come to think of as family. Marilyn Monroe preferred a secluded bungalow at the northern end of the property. Garbo, too, found perfect solitude here. Both Laurence Olivier and David Niven were among the British contingent of stars who preferred the Bel-Air. Bette Davis, when told by a studio limousine driver that the hotel was full, replied, "Take me to the Bel-Air. They'll find room." And she was right.

Under Joseph Drown's ownership, the Bel-Air established its reputation not just as a hotel for the rich and famous, but as a casual paradise where any visitor from the community or from out of town would be welcomed. Just as they had in the days of The Sycamores Tea Room, local residents would stop by for breakfast, lunch, or dinner, a cup of afternoon tea, or a late-night drink in the wood-paneled bar. The gently sloping lawn beside Swan Lake became one of Los Angeles' most coveted locations for exchanging wedding vows. Easter, Thanksgiving, Christmas: Every festive holiday and special occasion found its perfect Southern California setting at the Hotel Bel-Air.

That close relationship between the hotel, its staff, their guests, and the community has grown only stronger with the passage of time and the passing along of Alphonzo Bell's and Joseph Drown's visions. With Mr. Drown's death in 1982, the hotel was acquired by the Caroline Hunt Trust Estate of Dallas. The Sazale-Bel-Air Group acquired the hotel in June 1989.

In the early nineteen eighties, five leading interior designers were brought in to revitalize the look of every room, while maintaining the decades-old commitment to casual luxury. The hotel also added a wing of twenty-seven rooms and six suites at the northern end of the property—new buildings so sensitively attuned to the originals that many guests believe they date back to the 1940s.

It's that aura of timelessness, coupled with an unerring commitment to quality and service, that continues to endear the hotel to its guests, both long-standing and new. In a corner of the world where constant change is the norm, the Bel-Air endures as a landmark of particular distinction—a hotel that, in perfect detail and spirit, captures the very essence of life in Southern California.

SOUTHERN CALIFORNIA ENTERTAINING, BEL-AIR STYLE

The governing principles behind the Bel-Air's casual style are quality and service: to offer its guests the very best, presented simply, beautifully, and with a minimum of pretension or fuss.

You'll find these same, quintessentially Southern California factors applying in every aspect of the Bel-Air lifestyle, and they readily translate to entertaining in your own home, whether you're welcoming overnight houseguests or hosting a brunch, luncheon, tea, or dinner party. Here's a brief distillate:

EXTEND SIMPLE, HEARTFELT TOKENS OF WELCOME

Every guest arriving at the Bel-Air finds in the room a handwritten welcome from the manager; if they've stayed at the hotel before, the message offers a "welcome back." Along with the note comes a bowl of fresh fruit, a jar of dried fruit, and a vase of flowers; later in the afternoon, a complimentary Chinese tea basket arrives.

Such little kindnesses have a wonderfully pleasurable effect, and they are easily reproduced at home: a brief note on personal stationery, left on a bedside table, telling a guest how much he or she is welcome, a small plate of fragrant oranges, a little dish of chocolate peppermints, or a bowl of flowers fresh-picked from your garden.

ENJOY THE OUTDOORS

The Hotel Bel-Air makes the most of Southern California's year-round temperate climate, as you can see in many of the menus in this book—set at the swimming pool, in a secluded courtyard, in the herb garden, on the terrace, or beside Swan Lake.

This aspect of Southern California-style entertaining may not be easy to reproduce if you live in a climate where winter comes on in full force. But at least three or four months out of the year, people almost everywhere can enjoy the pleasure of dining outdoors. And even when the weather forbids, you can still capture the Bel-Air's style in spirit: moving a table close to a window that offers a charming vista, or even strategically placing a few houseplants in the dining room to create an indoor garden ambience.

MATCH YOUR TABLE SETTINGS TO THE MOOD OF THE MEAL

In recent years, the Bel-Air has begun to move away from the formal white china one finds in so many restaurant and hotel dining rooms. While that remains the basic china, the free spirit of Southern California has also seen beautiful tableware—from handmade, peasant-style pot-

A picnic at the beach is a treat, especially when the food is as luscious as this. For recipes, see pages 66-69.

The Hotel Bel-Air combines cuisines from all over the world with beautiful surroundings.

tery to elegant designer settings—gracing special dishes and special occasions, depending on their mood.

In the home, this translates to a simple guideline: Don't be afraid to be eclectic. By adding just the right serving piece, or presenting your dessert course on a particularly lively or colorful set of plates, you can introduce an exciting note of drama, style, or fun to your entertaining.

TAKE ADVANTAGE OF FRESH, HIGH-QUALITY INGREDIENTS

In true Southern California style, the Hotel Bel-Air's cuisine makes bold use of fresh produce, from delicate baby salad leaves that garnish some main-course plates, to the field peas that may form a background for breakfast eggs, to the startling blackberry salsa that garnishes sorbets.

Today, most cooks nationwide enjoy the same advantage as does the Hotel Bel-Air's kitchen, thanks to modern air freight that brings fresh, in-season produce from around the world to our doorsteps year-round. Outstanding greengrocers and supermarket produce sections are proliferating in large cities and small towns alike, and the challenge to the home cook lies not so much in locating specific ingredients as it does in seeking out and patronizing those purveyors who regularly offer the best-quality, most comprehensive selections.

EXPLORE THE BEST OF THE WORLD'S CUISINES

While the concept of the Pacific Rim, with Los Angeles as its American link, is relatively new, Southern California has long been America's melting pot—not just of Asian cultures, but also those of the many other peoples from around the nation and around the world who have made this part of the country their home.

That vital eclecticism is vividly reflected in the cooking at the Bel-Air. Indeed, the very presence of Japanese, Chinese, French, Italian, German, and other influences in the recipes you'll find on the following pages somehow makes them seem only more American.

Southern California-style cooking, as exemplified by the Hotel Bel-Air, is not afraid of new ingredients or new tastes. It welcomes them, embraces them, and incorporates them into a sound culinary foundation that always emphasizes good-quality ingredients, prepared in ways that highlight their natural flavors.

PRESENT FOODS WITH SIMPLICITY AND DRAMA

The best of Southern California cuisine calls for plate or platter presentations that are not overly labored or fussy, highlighting the natural beauty of quality ingredients. At the Hotel Bel-Air, you won't find much of the elaborate sauce-painting in which some contemporary chefs like to indulge, turning the plate into a canvas for edible works of art. Rather, foods are arranged simply, in pleasing patterns whose visual drama derives from the ways in which several contrasting ingredients are presented. Extra attention is paid to the height of the food on the plate, creating a three-dimensionality that may make as great a visual impact as how the food is arranged.

Creativity in the kitchen, as in other artistic pursuits, is never static, and over time the presentations of certain dishes may evolve. Which means to say that you should feel free to treat your own presentation of these recipes as works in progress, ready to adapt or change the way they are arranged depending on the kind and quality of ingredients available to you, how they look on your own tableware, and whatever your own creativity may dictate.

CELEBRATE AMERICAN WINES

American wines, particularly those produced in the California wine country, are finally garnering the worldwide recognition and acclaim they so justly deserve. And, not surprisingly, offering your guests California wines is a hallmark of Southern California entertaining.

The Hotel Bel-Air's wine list, numbering some two dozen pages and offering approximately six hundred different bottles, devotes almost half of its space to the products of California vineyards. Many of those are highlighted in the wine suggestions that accompany most of the menus in this book. These suggestions include explanations of why certain varieties and qualities of wine work particularly well with certain dishes. Rather than merely following the suggestions to the letter, feel free to use them as guidelines for beginning your own exploration of California wines.

CHAPTER ONE

BREAKFAST

ROMANTIC BREAKFAST
Serves 2

MORNING AT THE HOTEL BEL-AIR SEEMS MADE FOR ROMANCE. AND THIS SELECTION OF LIGHT, enticing dishes is just the sort of menu to begin the day with a feeling of sweet serenity, comfort, and delight.

If you make this menu at home for a special occasion, such as an anniversary or Valentine's Day, its appeal lies in how much of the work you can do in advance the night before—putting fresh fruits in the refrigerator to chill, making the field pea salsa and the biscuit dough. For an even greater Bel-Air touch, set a bed tray with elegant china and silver and a small vase of flowers. Only a few simple preparations remain to be done just before serving, barely interfering with the romantic mood you wish to conjure.

Wine suggestion:
If you wish to indulge for a truly special occasion, champagne is perfect. Choose a half-bottle from Krug, Veuve Clicquot's Yellow Label, or a fine California sparkler, such as Roederer Estate.

TROPICAL JUICE COCKTAIL

SLICED PAPAYA AND MELON

SCRAMBLED EGGS WITH AGED JACK CHEESE AND FIELD PEA-TOMATO SALSA

BAKED POTATO TOSSED WITH BELL PEPPERS

SOUR CREAM BISCUITS

CAFÉ PRESSÉ AND AUTUMN-PICKED DARJEELING WITH RAW SUGAR AND CREAM

THE POWER BREAKFAST

Serves 4

Wine suggestion:

Most power breakfasts will be alcohol-free. But if the breakfast is occasioned by, say, the closing of a major deal, you might want to pour a celebratory style of champagne such as Dom Rosé, Krug Clos de Mesnil, Cristal, or Salon Le Mesnil.

T HERE WAS A TIME NOT TOO LONG AGO WHEN THE TERM "POWER BREAKFAST" BROUGHT FORTH images of steak and eggs, hashed browns, and Bloody Marys—foods for true heavy hitters of the business world. But today's smart executives realize that good health and success go hand in hand. The typical power breakfast served in The Restaurant at Hotel Bel-Air exemplifies this lighter, no-nonsense approach: simple, delicious, fuss-free foods that start the day on the firmest footing possible.

Any of these dishes can be prepared very easily and quickly at home—or, for that matter, in a rudimentary office kitchen—to make your own quietly assertive statement of power.

FRESH-SQUEEZED BLOOD-ORANGE JUICE

OLD-FASHIONED OATMEAL WITH CHINA CINNAMON AND HONEY

HOME-BAKED RAISIN BREAD TOAST

SLICED "FINGERLING" RED BANANAS AND SEASONAL BERRIES

KENYAN AA COFFEE, SERVED BLACK

FRESH-SQUEEZED BLOOD ORANGE JUICE

Popular in the Mediterranean, blood oranges add their vibrant red-orange color to the sun-drenched breakfast table at the Bel-Air. They're generally in season from December through June; at other times of the year, substitute regular juice oranges.

Count on squeezing approximately 1 pound of oranges for each 6- to 8-ounce glass of juice; the yield will vary with the variety of blood orange, where it was grown, the time of year, and the weather. The Bel-Air kitchen favors the "Moro" variety, a seedless blood orange with excellent color and flavor.

If you like your fresh-squeezed juice chilled, put the oranges in the refrigerator the night before.

OLD-FASHIONED OATMEAL WITH CHINA CINNAMON AND HONEY

Starting the oatmeal in cold milk, and constant stirring while it cooks, produces a very rich taste and texture that are complemented by China cinnamon—a very rare, dark variety of the spice, which has an intense aroma and naturally sweet flavor. If you can't find it at your local gourmet store, substitute the finest cinnamon available.

3   cups cold lowfat milk

1   cup rolled oats

½   cup honey

⅓   teaspoon salt

1   teaspoon ground China cinnamon

Put the milk, oats, ¼ cup of the honey, and the salt in a medium saucepan and cook over low heat, stirring constantly, until thick and creamy, about 6 minutes.

Ladle into serving bowls, dust to taste with cinnamon, and drizzle to taste with the remaining honey. If you like, accompany the oatmeal with a small china pitcher of warm milk, to be added to taste.

HOME-BAKED RAISIN BREAD TOAST

Generously filled with raisins and flavored with a little molasses, this rich loaf is one of the great treats on the Bel-Air's breakfast menu.

The secret to its superb taste and texture is the dough's long, slow proofing in the refrigerator—for three full days—which breaks down the raisins slightly and blends their flavor into the bread. (Diced dried figs substituted for the raisins is an excellent variation.)

If you can't wait 3 days, proof the dough in the more common way, in a loosely covered bowl at room temperature for a few hours, until doubled in bulk; then punch it down and let it rise a second time. The resulting bread won't be the authentic Bel-Air product, but it will still taste good.

Bake the bread the afternoon or evening before you plan to toast it for breakfast. Cut it with a bread knife into slices about ½ inch thick. The importance of toasting the bread just before serving can't be emphasized too much: It's best appreciated while still hot and crisp. To ensure this, the Bel-Air includes a plug-in toaster with all of its room service breakfasts, so guests can prepare their raisin bread toast the moment they want it.

This recipe makes one 1½-pound loaf, which will keep well for 2 to 3 days in a plastic bag in the refrigerator.

3   cups bread flour

1   cup seedless dark raisins

1   tablespoon active dried yeast (1 packet)

2   teaspoons salt

¾   cup cold water

4   tablespoons molasses

In the bowl of an electric mixer with a dough hook (or in a large mixing bowl, using a large spoon or your hands), combine the flour, raisins, yeast, and salt. Add the water and molasses, and knead the dough with the hook—or on a floured surface with your hands—until smooth and elastic, about 10 minutes.

Cover the bowl securely with plastic wrap, and leave it in the coldest part of the refrigerator for 3 days.

Uncover the dough and punch it down. Return it to the mixer and knead with the dough hook—or by hand on a floured surface—for about 5 more minutes.

Empty the dough onto a floured work surface and shape it into an oblong loaf. Place it in a greased 2-quart (9 x 4-inch) loaf pan, cover loosely with a kitchen towel, and let rise at room temperature until doubled in bulk, about 1 hour.

Place a baking pan on the oven floor, and preheat the oven to 400 degrees F. Put the risen loaf in the oven and, being extremely careful to avoid the steam, immediately pour ½ cup of water into the baking pan at the bottom of the oven.

Bake the bread until it is well risen and golden and sounds hollow when rapped with a knuckle, about 40 minutes; do not open the oven door during the first 20 minutes of baking. Cool to room temperature on a wire rack before slicing.

SLICED "FINGERLING" RED BANANAS AND SEASONAL BERRIES

A small banana farm in Southern California, on the coast just south of Santa Barbara, produces outstanding, rare varieties of the fruit—including sweet, tiny red-skinned ones known at the Bel-Air as "fingerlings," referring to their dainty size. Sliced diagonally and arranged on a platter or on individual plates with generous amounts of seasonal berries, they make a striking breakfast presentation.

Many gourmet markets and produce stands carry an ever-growing number of banana varieties. If you can't find small red-skinned ones, substitute the bananas that are sweetest and most perfectly ripe without being overly soft.

KENYAN AA COFFEE, SERVED BLACK

Full-bodied and marvelously smooth, with a mild, delicate trace of acidity, AA-grade Kenyan coffee is one of the world's finest. Yet it is widely available at most coffee stores and at gourmet shops specializing in varietal beans.

For breakfast, a dark—but not too dark—"full-city" roast is recommended to show off the coffee's richness without overwhelming the still-wakening palate. Brew it by the drip method and serve it black; cream or sugar are superfluities not in keeping with the no-nonsense, healthful, power breakfast mentality.

Blood Orange Juice. Old-Fashioned Oatmeal with China Cinnamon and Honey. Home-Baked Raisin Bread Toast.

Après-Workout Poolside Breakfast

Serves 1

EARLY IN THE MORNING, THE SWIMMING POOL AT THE BEL-AIR IS A HAVEN OF SERENITY: THE PERFECT spot for solitary lap swimming, followed by a supremely healthy breakfast delivered on a tray to your chaise-side table. Slip on a luxurious white terry robe, sit back and read the morning papers from both coasts, and enjoy a delicious and invigorating start to the day.

Each dish in this menu is so easily prepared that you may well have the illusion it was delivered to you on a tray after your own daily workout. The frappé ingredients are simply popped into the blender or food processor. The granola is made in quantity, ready to eat at a moment's notice. And the yogurt, too, is made in advance—following the instructions given here, or by your favorite dairy.

Wine suggestion:

While one doesn't really think of drinking wine at an after-workout breakfast, you might want to seek out a comparable healthy experience: the outstanding nonalcoholic Gewürztraminer grape juice now being produced by Navarro Winery in Mendocino County, California.

STRAWBERRY-MANGO YOGURT FRAPPÉ

HOMEMADE VANILLA-BEAN YOGURT

BEL-AIR GRANOLA

BLACK COFFEE OR TEA

STRAWBERRY-MANGO YOGURT FRAPPÉ

Frothy and thick, this fresh fruit drink is a favorite breakfast item of health-conscious guests at the Bel-Air.

2   medium-size ripe strawberries, stemmed

¼   cup (about ¼ medium-size) very ripe mango, peeled

¼   cup plain lowfat yogurt

3   tablespoons club soda

1   teaspoon sugar

Put all the ingredients in a blender or food processor and blend until smooth and frothy. Serve immediately.

HOMEMADE VANILLA-BEAN YOGURT

Starting the night before you plan to serve it, it's very easy to make your own yogurt at home, especially with the help of one of the reasonably priced yogurt makers found at most well-equipped cookware shops.

To get it started, you'll need some nonpasteurized plain yogurt, that is, one containing live yogurt cultures; or you could substitute powdered yogurt culture (following label directions), available at health food stores. Alternatively, serve your favorite brand of vanilla yogurt.

The quantities given here yield enough for 4 or 5 servings, which will keep well in the refrigerator for several days.

1   quart whole or lowfat milk

2   vanilla beans

½   cup plain, nonpasteurized whole-milk or lowfat yogurt, at room temperature

Pour the milk in a medium saucepan. With a sharp knife, carefully split the vanilla-bean pods; with the knife tip, scrape the pulp from inside the pods into the milk, and add the pods as well. Bring the milk to a boil, and remove it from the heat immediately.

Let the milk cool at room temperature to 110 degrees F on a cooking thermometer. Remove the vanilla-bean pods. Stir a little of the warm milk into the yogurt to liquefy it, then gently stir the yogurt into the pan of milk.

Pour the yogurt mixture into a home yogurt maker and incubate overnight. Serve straight from the yogurt maker, or refrigerate before serving.

BEL-AIR GRANOLA

Granola lovers really enjoy the mixture served at the Bel-Air. The generous quantities given here make enough for twenty ½-cup servings, which will keep well stored in airtight containers at cool room temperature. If you like, you can cut the ingredients by half or more, to yield enough to suit your own needs.

3   cups uncooked whole-grain cereal

1½   cups wheat germ

¾   cup oat bran

¾   cup shelled Macadamia nuts, coarsely chopped or crushed

¾   cup shelled pecans, coarsely chopped

¾   cup blanched almond slices

¾   cup shelled sunflower seeds

¾   cup honey

1   cup flavorless vegetable oil

½   tablespoon pure vanilla extract

1   tablespoon ground cinnamon

½   tablespoon grated nutmeg

1   cup toasted shredded coconut

In a large mixing bowl, combine the grains, nuts, and sunflower seeds. Add the honey, oil, vanilla, and spices to the bowl, and rub the mixture between your palms until thoroughly coated.

Spread the mixture evenly in a thin layer on sheet pans, and toast slowly in an oven set to 225 degrees F until golden brown, about 2½ hours.

Remove from the oven, cool to room temperature, and toss thoroughly with the coconut. Store in airtight containers.

Serve plain, with fresh fruit, or with milk or yogurt.

BLACK COFFEE OR TEA

If you still feel the need for caffeine after your revitalizing morning workout, prepare your favorite variety of coffee or tea and serve it—black, of course—from an individual china or porcelain pot. An alternative would be choosing an herbal tea from the large variety available.

Poolside refreshments.

CHAPTER TWO

BRUNCH

Family Brunch on a Private Terrace

Serves 6

WEEKEND BRUNCH AT HOTEL BEL-AIR IS A FAVORITE WAY TO CELEBRATE A FAMILY OCCASION—BE it a birthday, a wedding anniversary, or another special day. Whether served on The Terrace or on one of the secluded, private terraces adjoining a suite of rooms, the occasion is made even more festive by nearby halos of pink bougainvillea and by the distant music of the hotel's fountains.

The beauty of serving this menu at home is how little cooking you actually have to do. Though the Bel-Air makes its own highly acclaimed smoked salmon, that process requires work, time, and equipment beyond the scope of most accomplished home chefs; you are well advised to buy the best smoked salmon available. The same advice goes for the basket of assorted breads. Place all of these prepared-in-advance dishes on the table just before guests arrive, for service buffet style. The only cooking and individual-plate presentation you need do is for the French toast sandwiches and the accompanying bacon—minimal work for such a strikingly beautiful presentation, well befitting a celebration—which leaves the cook free to join in the festivities.

If the weather is nice, plan to serve the meal on your own terrace or patio. If this is not possible, move the table near a window to enjoy the view and the fresh air.

Fresh Fruit Juices or Mimosas

Sally Lunn French Toast Sandwiches with Strawberry Compote and Mascarpone

Assorted Sliced Melons and Whole Fresh Berries

Smoked Salmon with Chive Cream Cheese and Bagels

Applewood-Smoked Bacon

Basket of Assorted Breads

Coffee and Tea

Wine suggestion:
The smoked salmon in this menu calls for a fruity, dry white wine that you can drink with the other dishes as well. One excellent choice is Zind-Humbuct "Hengst Vineyard" Gewürztraminer from Alsace, France—an excellent wine well worth seeking out. Or you might want to try a somewhat sweeter California Gewürztraminer, such as those from Fetzer or Beringer. For an extra-special occasion, such as a birthday brunch, break out your favorite champagne.

FRESH FRUIT JUICES OR MIMOSAS

Set out pitchers of two or more different fresh-squeezed, chilled fruit juices or juice blends and an array of glasses, allowing guests to help themselves.

If the occasion warrants, you might wish to offer an option of mimosas: fresh orange juice mixed fifty-fifty with iced champagne or sparkling wine.

SALLY LUNN FRENCH TOAST SANDWICHES WITH STRAWBERRY COMPOTE AND MASCARPONE

Elegant and delicious, these brunch sandwiches are very easy to make. Bake the Sally Lunn—a rich egg bread—a day or two before; or substitute the best egg bread you can find, whether a French-style brioche or a Jewish challah, from your local bakery. The compote can be quickly prepared the night before and refrigerated, to be taken out and brought to room temperature when you start putting the meal together.

Mascarpone, a thick and tangy Italian-style cream, is available in Italian delis or gourmet markets; you may substitute whipped cream.

STRAWBERRY COMPOTE

1   cup large strawberries, cut in halves

1   cup whole small strawberries (or, if unavailable, the same quantity of large strawberries cut in half)

⅔   cup sugar

1   tablespoon brandy

1   teaspoon grated orange zest

Stir together all the ingredients in a bowl. Cover with plastic wrap and refrigerate. Remove from the refrigerator about 1 hour before making the sandwiches, allowing the compote to come to room temperature.

FRENCH TOAST

8   eggs

¾   cup milk

1   teaspoon pure vanilla extract

½   teaspoon grated nutmeg

12   ½-inch-thick slices Sally Lunn or other rich egg bread, trimmed to 3-inch squares

¾   cup mascarpone, chilled, or chilled whipped cream

Confectioner's sugar

6   sprigs fresh mint

Zest of 2 oranges, julienned and simmered for 10 minutes in a syrup of 1 cup each water and sugar, then removed and dried on a sugared plate (optional)

Beat the eggs together with the milk, vanilla, and nutmeg in a large mixing bowl. Put the bread slices in the bowl, and gently turn them until they are saturated with the mixture.

Heat a lightly greased or nonstick griddle or pan over medium heat. Lift the slices from the egg mixture, let excess liquid drip off, and place them on the griddle, in batches if necessary; cook until golden brown, about 3 minutes per side. Keep warm.

To assemble the sandwiches, put 1 slice of French toast on each serving plate. Top with ⅓ cup of the compote then ¼ cup of mascarpone. Dust a second slice of toast with confectioner's sugar and place on top. Garnish with mint sprigs and candied orange zest.

SALLY LUNN BREAD

The name of this rich egg bread comes from an eighteenth-century pastry cook in Bath, England, who popularized what was most likely a far-older recipe.

Make the bread a day ahead of time for French toast. These quantities will yield one 1-pound loaf.

STARTER

7   ounces milk

2   tablespoons all-purpose flour

¾   teaspoon sugar

1   tablespoon active dried yeast (1 packet)

In a mixing bowl, stir together ingredients until the yeast has dissolved completely. Set aside at warm room temperature for 20 minutes.

DOUGH INGREDIENTS

3   cups bread flour

3   tablespoons softened unsalted butter

2   tablespoons sugar

¾   teaspoon salt

1   egg

Finely grated zest of ½ lemon

Pinch of nutmeg

In an electric mixer with a dough hook (for hand-kneading instructions, see page 30), combine the starter with the remaining dough ingredients and knead until the dough forms a ball. Cover the bowl with plastic wrap and leave at warm room temperature to rise until doubled in bulk, about 45 minutes.

Punch down the dough and put it into a 2-quart (9 x 4-inch) loaf pan. Cover with plastic wrap and leave it to rise until doubled in bulk, about 45 minutes.

Place a baking pan on the oven floor and preheat the oven to 350 degrees F. Put the risen loaf in the oven and, being extremely careful to avoid the steam, immediately pour ½ cup of water into the baking pan at the bottom of the oven.

Bake the loaf until it is well-risen and golden and sounds hollow when rapped with a knuckle, 35 to 40 minutes; do not open the oven door during the first 20 minutes of baking. Cool to room temperature on a wire rack.

ASSORTED SLICED MELONS AND WHOLE FRESH BERRIES

This casual presentation of fresh seasonal fruit encourages guests to help themselves throughout the brunch.

Buy two or three different kinds of melons and chill them; halve them, scoop out the seeds, and then cut them into thin slices or wedges. Arrange the slices in an attractive pattern on a serving platter with whole, fresh, seasonal berries.

Sally Lunn French Toast Sandwiches with Strawberry Compote and Mascarpone

SMOKED SALMON WITH CHIVE CREAM CHEESE AND BAGELS

It's an enjoyable task to methodically purchase and sample a few ounces of smoked salmon from your local gourmet market or deli, arriving at your own choice of the best available. You can do the same for bagels, finding the kind that best suit your taste.

Plan on about 2 ounces of smoked salmon per person, and ask that it be cut into long, thin slices on the bias. Though guests will average about 1 regular-size or 2 miniature bagels each, you might want to buy a dozen large or 2 dozen small ones just so you can offer a variety—water, egg, sesame, poppy seed, onion, or some of the other flavors now commonly available.

Before serving, arrange the salmon slices over-lapping on a platter and garnish with fresh lemon slices or wedges. Split the bagels and toast them, presenting them in a bread basket or on a platter. Offer cream cheese—about ¾ cup—whipped with a generous amount of freshly chopped chives, for guests to spread on their bagels before topping with salmon and seasoning with a squeeze of lemon.

APPLEWOOD-SMOKED BACON

Bacon that has been cured over applewood embers has an incomparably sweet and smoky taste that com-plements the natural flavor of the pork itself. Mis-souri and Wisconsin are the preeminent producers of this kind of bacon, which you can probably track down in a good gourmet market; if not, substitute the best smoked slab bacon you can find.

Though most Americans prefer their bacon ultracrisp, thick-cut slab bacon is really at its best if cooked until well browned but still chewy.

Serve this bacon as a side dish to the French toast sandwiches, starting its cooking around the time you begin to griddle-cook the French toast.

1½   pounds whole-slab applewood-smoked bacon,
rind trimmed, cut into ¼-inch-thick slices

Preheat the oven to 350 degrees F. Place the bacon strips side by side in a baking pan, and put the pan in the oven. Bake until the bacon is nicely browned but not yet crisp, about 10 minutes.

Drain on paper towels and serve immediately.

BASKET OF ASSORTED BREADS

All over the nation, in large cities and small towns alike, there seems to be a resurgence of the art of baking. Good bakeries are springing up everywhere, offering a wide variety of loaves, rolls, croissants, and muffins; and though the Bel-Air bakes most of its own breads, the kitchen staff also regularly reviews the best new products from Los Angeles bakers for service as table breads in the restaurant.

For this brunch, assemble an assortment of breads—particularly individual rolls, croissants, and muffins—from your own favorite local bakery. Warm them in a low oven before serving, and present them in a napkin-lined basket, accompanied by butter and a variety of jams.

COFFEE AND TEA

Brew a large pot of your favorite morningtime coffee. Have water ready to boil for individual cups or small pots of tea, presenting a variety of options—English breakfast, Darjeeling, Irish breakfast, orange pekoe, and assorted herbal teas.

Brunch on The Terrace

Picnic Brunch in the Herb Garden
Serves 10 to 12

T UCKED AWAY BEHIND THE BUILDINGS OF CHALONE COURT, THE BEL-AIR HERB GARDEN IS A singular haven within the hotel's peaceful environs. Sunshine radiates warmly in the open space, summoning forth the heady aromas of fresh basil, oregano, lemon thyme, and a host of other herbs. This setting is the starting point for the following menu. Not surprisingly, with such an abundance of fresh herbs, the menu is unabashedly Mediterranean—both in its flavors and in its decidedly relaxed buffet style of service.

You can take a similarly relaxed approach to preparing the menu yourself: Each dish lends itself to preparation the night before the picnic and is easy to pack in airtight containers if your picnic is any farther than your own back garden; each dish is simple and straightforward to present. The recipes double or halve easily if you wish to invite more or fewer guests. And, to make the work even easier, you might like to plan the picnic with your friends, sending each participant a photocopy of the particular recipe you would like them to bring along.

Wine suggestion:

The strong, distinctive flavors in this menu call for wines with a nice acidic balance to them that cleanse the palate with each sip. Offer 3 different varieties of wine, to suit guests' different preferences and to complement the different courses: a dryish, lighter white wine with a good acid backbone, such as a Sauvignon (also known as Fumé) Blanc from Matanzas Creek, Iron Horse, Silverado, or Fetzer; a fuller, dryish Chardonnay, such as Sonoma Cutrer "Russian River," Trefethen, Semi, or Matanzas Creek; and, for the red wine (served cool), choose any Beaujolais imported by DeBoeuf or a California Pinot Noir—especially Saintsbury "Garnet."

GRILLED EGGPLANT WITH CURRIED PEPPERS AND PENNE SALAD

COUNTRY-STYLE PORK SHOULDER BRAISED WITH ONIONS AND OLIVES

VINE-RIPENED RED AND GOLD TOMATOES WITH FRESH HERBS AND MARINATED BOCCONCINI

SLICED EGGS AND PESTO TOAST WITH PRAWNS STEAMED IN THE SHELL

FRESH FRUIT AND CHEESES

CROISSANTS, CORNBREAD, AND ROSEMARY FLATBREAD

CHILLED WINE, COFFEE, HERBAL TEA, AND JUICES

The herb garden at the Hotel Bel-Air inspired these delicious recipes.

SLICED EGGS AND PESTO TOAST WITH PRAWNS STEAMED IN THE SHELL

Here's a wonderfully casual combination of picnic items that just seem to go together: toasts spread with fresh basil pesto and topped with hard-boiled eggs, and large prawns, fragrantly steamed in their shells and cooled.

You can do virtually all of the work the night before, blending the pesto, boiling the eggs, and steaming the prawns. Make the toast shortly beforehand, and then assemble everything just before serving.

STEAMED PRAWNS

½   cup extra virgin olive oil

4   tablespoons balsamic vinegar

3   tablespoons chopped fresh thyme

2   tablespoon finely chopped garlic

2   teaspoons salt

1   teaspoon freshly ground black pepper

     Grated zest of 4 lemons

24   large uncooked prawns in the shell, with heads intact

6   bay leaves

Stir together the oil, vinegar, and all seasonings except the bay leaves in a large mixing bowl. Add the prawns, toss well to coat them, cover, and marinate in the refrigerator for 3 hours.

Fill the bottom of a steamer with several inches of water, and add the bay leaves. Bring to a boil and simmer briskly for 10 minutes. Raise the heat and add the prawns to the steamer basket, keeping them tightly covered. Steam for 4 minutes. Remove the prawns from the heat and spread them on a shallow tray to cool in their shells. Then put them and the juices that collect into a bowl, cover, and refrigerate.

SLICED EGGS ON PESTO TOAST

12   eggs

1   cup fresh basil leaves

¼   cup grated Parmesan cheese

3   tablespoons toasted pine nuts

3 to 4 medium garlic cloves, finely chopped

     Juice of 1 lemon

½ to ¾ cup olive oil

1   teaspoon salt

½   teaspoon white pepper

12   slices white sandwich bread, crusts trimmed

For perfect hard-boiled eggs, with the yolks still somewhat moist at the center, put the eggs in a large saucepan and add cold water to cover. Cover the pan and bring the water to a boil; then remove from the heat, and let the eggs sit for 4 minutes. Drain well, cover the eggs with cold water, and let them cool. Refrigerate until ready to serve.

For the pesto, process the basil, Parmesan, pine nuts, and lemon juice in a blender or food processor until very finely chopped. With the motor running, very slowly pour in the oil, adding enough to form a smooth, thick emulsion. Stir in the seasonings, transfer to a bowl, cover with plastic wrap, and refrigerate.

Before serving, toast the bread until golden and crisp. Spread each slice with pesto, then cut each piece of toast in half diagonally. Peel the eggs and cut each in half lengthwise, placing them in the center of a large platter.

Arrange the toasts around the rim of a platter. Drain the prawns and leave them in their shells, or shell them, as you wish; arrange them on the platter.

FRESH FRUIT AND CHEESES

An abundant assortment of fresh seasonal fruits and fine cheeses contributes to the festive air of any picnic. Transport and present the fruits whole, placing them on a bowl or on a platter for guests to help themselves.

Select and offer large blocks or wedges of at least 3 different cheeses, such as an aged Cheddar, a good Gruyère, a fresh or aged goat cheese, a creamy ripe Brie or Camembert—whatever looks best and most appealing at your local deli or market. Arrange them on a platter or on a wooden carving board.

CROISSANTS, CORNBREAD, AND ROSEMARY FLATBREAD

A generous selection of breads is essential to the picnic—for guests to nibble alone, to sop up salad dressing, to make pork sandwiches, or to eat with a slice or spread of cheese. Buy a fresh-baked selection from your local bakery—including the rosemary flatbread known as "focaccia," which has become a featured item at Italian bakeries across the country. If you want to include a pan of fresh-baked corn bread, follow your own favorite recipe or the one given as part of the stuffing recipe on page 134.

CHILLED WINE, COFFEE, HERBAL TEA, AND JUICES

Bring along bags of ice and some ice buckets for the wines suggested at the beginning of this menu. In addition to the wines, prepare thermoses of hot coffee and herbal teas, and bring bottles or jugs of fresh fruit juice—and, perhaps, some sparkling water—to slake the thirst.

Brunch by the Fire

Serves 4

EVEN IN SOUTHERN CALIFORNIA, FALL AND WINTER MORNINGS CAN FIND A CHILL IN THE AIR, AND the sheltered seclusion of Stone Canyon can intensify the desire to draw close to the fireside and enjoy a brunch of warming, comforting foods. This cold-weather weekend menu celebrates dishes and ingredients associated with the season, from Apple-Pear Cider to a dish of poached eggs accompanied by a warm salad of wild mushrooms to freshly baked muffins that all but explode with the color and flavor of persimmons and cranberries.

With its baking, frying, and sautéing, this menu takes a little more work than some, though much of the preparation can be done in advance. But on a cold weekend morning, the kitchen is as welcoming a place to be as the fireside. If your kitchen is large enough, in fact, you might even want to consider serving this brunch there.

Wine suggestion:

A cold day and the robust flavors of the menu call for heartier wines. If you want to pour a white, choose a rich and oakey Chardonnay, such as Chalone, Mondavi Reserve, Simi Reserve, or Montelena. Or you could select a French white Burgundy, such as a Montrachet or Meursault. For a red wine, opt for a rich California Pinot Noir such as Calera, Mondavi Reserve, or Acacia "St. Clair."

GRAVENSTEIN APPLE-PEAR CIDER

POACHED EGGS WITH A WARM SALAD OF MUSHROOMS, GRIDDLED PEAMEAL PORK LOIN, SPINACH, AND BALSAMIC VINAIGRETTE

ASSORTED FRUIT FRITTERS WITH MAPLE-GINGER CRÈME FRAÎCHE

MULTIGRAIN TOAST WITH TREACLE BUTTER

PERSIMMON AND CRANBERRY MUFFINS

POTATO AND ONION PIE

HOT TEA AND COCOA

GRAVENSTEIN APPLE-PEAR CIDER

Apple and pear juices combine in this mellow, richly perfumed nectar, the perfect start for a cold-weather brunch.

Tart and spicy in flavor, the Gravenstein is a fine juice apple whose growing season extends into early autumn. If it is unavailable, you might want to substitute such varieties as Mcintosh, Jonathan, Northern Spy, Spartan, Winesap, or Delicious. For the pears, select a juicy variety such as Bartlett or Comice.

You'll need an electric, liquifier-type juicer—the kind you often see at health food juice bars—to make the cider. If you wish, you can achieve a similar—though less fresh-tasting—result by combining natural, unfiltered apple and pear juices from a local health food market.

The quantities given here make about 1½ quarts. Any leftover juice will keep well in the refrigerator for several days.

12   ripe Gravenstein apples, peeled, cored, and cut into chunks

3   ripe pears, peeled, cored, and cut into chunks

Process the pieces of fruit together in an electric juice extractor. Transfer to a bottle or pitcher, cover, and refrigerate until serving.

The juice's solids will settle over time. If you want a clearer juice, pour carefully as you would to decant a wine; if you want a thicker, natural-looking juice, stir before pouring.

POACHED EGGS WITH A WARM SALAD OF MUSHROOMS, GRIDDLED PEAMEAL PORK LOIN, SPINACH, AND BALSAMIC VINAIGRETTE

Light and flavorful, this recipe combines the best attributes of a classic brunch egg dish and a warm spinach salad. You can vary the kinds of mushrooms you use in the dish, depending on what is available at your market. Peameal pork loin is a wonderfully sweet and savory type of cured loin bacon; if unavailable, substitute Canadian bacon or slices of a good, meaty, cured ham.

Much of the dish's preparation—sautéing the mushrooms, searing the pork, poaching the eggs—is done quickly at the last minute. The key to effortless cooking is to have all the ingredients prepared and arranged, ready to combine. The one thing you can make ahead is the vinaigrette.

BALSAMIC VINAIGRETTE

1½   tablespoons olive oil

½   tablespoon balsamic vinegar

½   tablespoon finely chopped shallots

¼   teaspoon salt

Pinch of white pepper

Stir together all the ingredients. Cover and set aside.

WARM SALAD OF MUSHROOMS

4   tablespoons olive oil

½   cup pearl onions, peeled

1   cup chanterelle mushrooms, cut into ¼-inch-thick slices

½   cup cremini mushrooms, cut into ¼-inch-thick slices

2   tablespoons water

½   cup oyster mushrooms, cut into ¼-inch-thick slices

½   cup shiitake mushrooms, cut into ¼-inch-thick slices

¼   cup scallions, sliced thinly on the bias

1   tablespoon chopped shallots

1   tablespoon chopped fresh parsley

1   teaspoon chopped fresh thyme

1   teaspoon salt

½   teaspoon white pepper

¼   cup dry white wine

½   cup seeded and diced tomatoes

1   cup white vinegar

8   eggs

4   very thin slices peameal pork loin

1¾   cups baby spinach leaves, loosely packed

¾   cup curly endive, loosely packed

Salt to taste

Freshly ground black pepper to taste

Heat 1 tablespoon of the oil in a large skillet over moderate heat and sauté the onions until tender and light golden, about 3 minutes. Remove them from the skillet.

Add the remaining oil to the skillet, and raise the heat to high. Add the chanterelles and creminis and sauté for 20 seconds. Add the water and the remaining mushrooms, the onions, scallions, shallots, herbs, salt, and pepper; sauté 20 seconds. Immediately add the wine and simmer briskly until the liquid in the skillet reduces to a thick essence, 2 to 3 minutes. Remove the skillet from the heat, add the tomatoes, toss to combine, and set aside.

In a wide, deep pan, bring 3 quarts of water to a boil. At the same time, heat a nonstick skillet or griddle over moderate heat. Add the white vinegar to the water and, one at a time, very carefully break the eggs into the boiling water, holding their shells close to the surface; poach just until the whites are firm, about 2 minutes, removing them with a slotted spoon to drain on a kitchen towel. At the same time, put the pork loin slices on the skillet or griddle and sear them on each side just until a little color develops, about 1½ minutes per side.

To assemble the dishes, distribute the mushroom mixture evenly on serving plates. Toss the spinach and endive with the vinaigrette, season with salt and pepper, and mound the leaves in the middle of each plate. Drape a slice of pork alongside the leaves, and place 2 poached eggs at the bottom of each plate.

Poached Eggs with a Warm Salad of Mushrooms, Griddled Peameal Pork Loin, Spinach, and Balsamic Vinaigrette

ASSORTED FRUIT FRITTERS WITH MAPLE-GINGER CRÈME FRAÎCHE

Dipped in a light, cinnamon-spiced batter and deep-fried, these fritters of fresh fruit make a delightful brunch appetizer on a chilly day.

Feel free to vary the kinds of fruit you use, depending on what looks best at your market, but steer clear of especially delicate or juicy fruits such as berries or melons. Make and refrigerate the crème fraîche a day in advance. Gather together all the other ingredients shortly before guests arrive. Then, just before everyone sits down, start heating the oil and mix up the batter. Dust, dip, and fry the fruit just before serving.

MAPLE-GINGER CRÈME FRAÎCHE

1	cup heavy cream
¼	cup buttermilk
5	ounces maple syrup
½	tablespoon juice squeezed from grated fresh ginger root

Stir together the cream and buttermilk in a mixing bowl. Cover with plastic wrap and leave at warm room temperature for 12 hours. Then stir in the maple syrup and ginger juice and refrigerate until serving.

FRUIT FRITTERS

1	quart vegetable oil
1	cup cornstarch
¾	cup cake flour
1	teaspoon baking soda
1	teaspoon ground cinnamon
1	cup iced water
2	egg whites
4	seedless orange segments
1	ripe banana, peeled and cut on the bias into 4 pieces
1	ripe red plum, pitted and quartered
½	pear, peeled, seeded, and cut on the bias into 4 pieces
½	tart apple, peeled, seeded, and cut on the bias into 4 pieces
¼	ripe papaya, peeled, seeded, and cut on the bias into 4 pieces

Heat the oil in a deep fryer or a heavy 2-quart pot that is taller than it is wide, to a temperature of 350 degrees F on a deep-frying thermometer.

While the oil is heating, make the batter. In a mixing bowl, stir together ¾ cup of cornstarch with the flour, baking soda, and cinnamon. In a separate bowl, combine the water and egg whites, then add them all at once to the dry ingredients, stirring just until blended; the batter should be slightly lumpy.

When the oil is hot, lightly dust the fruit pieces with the remaining cornstarch. One at a time, dip each piece in the batter and, without shaking off any excess, carefully drop it directly into the oil; repeat with remaining pieces. Fry the fritters until golden brown, 3 to 4 minutes, removing each piece with a wire skimmer when done and transferring it to paper towels to drain.

Serve immediately, accompanied by crème fraîche.

MULTIGRAIN TOAST WITH TREACLE BUTTER

Toast made from a healthy and hearty multigrain loaf seems a perfect addition to a cold-weather brunch. If you don't want to go to the trouble of baking the loaf given here, seek out the best locally baked multigrain bread you can find. Slice the bread ½ inch thick for toasting, and toast it fresh for guests just before serving.

The spiced treacle butter is an especially wholesome-tasting topping for the toast, and can be made well in advance and refrigerated; just be sure to take it out of the refrigerator in time for it to soften to spreadable consistency. Treacle is a by-product of the sugar refining process. It resembles molasses, which is an acceptable substitute.

MULTIGRAIN BREAD

3	cups bread flour
½	cup rye flour
½	cup oat bran
½	cup wheat bran
¼	cup sesame seeds
¼	cup millet
¼	cup shelled sunflower seeds, crushed
1	tablespoon kosher salt
2	packets active dry yeast
¾	cup warm water
⅓	cup honey
¼	cup peanut oil
2	tablespoons thick soy sauce

BREAD TOPPING

¼	cup rolled oats
3	tablespoons sesame seeds
3	tablespoons shelled sunflower seeds

In the bowl of an electric mixer with a dough hook, combine all the flours, brans, grains, and seeds. Stir in the salt.

Stir the yeast into the water, and leave at room temperature about 10 minutes to activate. With the mixer running on its slowest speed, pour the yeast into the flour mixture, then add the honey, peanut oil, and soy. Continue mixing as you gradually add enough of the remaining water to make a firm, not-too-sticky dough. Knead the dough until smooth and elastic, about 10 minutes. (For hand-kneading instructions, see page 30.)

Cover the bowl securely with plastic wrap, and leave it at warm room temperature until doubled in bulk, about 1½ hours. Punch the dough down, divide it in 2, and shape into round loaves. Toss together the grains for the bread's topping, and gently roll the top of each round in the mixture to coat it.

Place the loaves on a flour-dusted baking sheet, cover with plastic wrap, and leave at warm room temperature until doubled in bulk again, about 1 hour.

Place a baking pan on the oven floor, and preheat the oven to 375 degrees F. Put the risen loaves in the oven and, being extremely careful to avoid the steam, immediately pour ½ cup of water into the baking pan at the bottom of the oven.

Bake the loaves until they are well risen and golden, and sound hollow when rapped with a knuckle, about 45 minutes; do not open the oven door during the first 20 minutes of baking. Cool to room temperature on a wire rack before slicing and toasting.

TREACLE BUTTER

1   pound unsalted butter, at cool room
     temperature

½ to ¾ cup treacle

     Grated zest of 1 orange

2   teaspoons ground cinnamon

1   teaspoon grated nutmeg

⅛   teaspoon ground cloves

Put the butter in a food processor with the metal blade, and process until whipped smoothly. With the machine running, gradually pour in the treacle; add the remaining ingredients and process until blended. Transfer to a bowl, cover, and refrigerate until about 30 minutes before serving.

PERSIMMON AND CRANBERRY MUFFINS

Fresh-baked muffins are a wonderfully warming touch for brunch. Vividly colored and flavored with fruits that speak to us of the chilly season, these are deliciously served hot from the oven just as they are, or with sweet butter. Present them in a napkin-lined basket or bowl.

The recipe makes about 16 muffins. Leftovers, once cooled, may be frozen in airtight bags, to be gently reheated in the oven or microwave.

2   cups brown sugar

6   tablespoons unsalted butter

6   eggs

3¼   cups pastry flour

3   tablespoons baking powder

1   teaspoon ground cinnamon

½   teaspoon grated nutmeg

½   cup orange juice

¾   cup whole cranberries

6   ripe persimmons, peeled, pitted, and diced
     into ¼-inch pieces

Preheat the oven to 350 degrees F. In a mixing bowl, cream together the sugar and butter until very light in texture and color. One at a time, beat in the eggs. In a separate bowl, combine the flour, baking powder, and spices, then gradually stir them into the creamed mixture, alternating with splashes of orange juice. Add the remaining ingredients and stir just until thoroughly combined.

Spoon the mixture into a greased muffin tin, filling the cups about ¾ full, and bake until the muffins are well-risen and golden, about 25 minutes. Allow the muffins to cool in the tin before unmolding.

POTATO AND ONION PIE

This rustic elaboration of a potato pancake makes a perfect accompaniment to the poached egg dish. A few hours in advance you can perform all the steps up to, but not including, the final assembly and baking. Then put the pie together and pop it in the oven as guests sit down to the meal.

4   tablespoons olive oil

1½   medium white onions, thinly sliced

½   cup water

2   teaspoons salt

½   teaspoon freshly ground black pepper

2   medium baking potatoes

8   Kalamata or Niçoise black olives, pitted

4   sprigs fresh rosemary

Heat half the oil in a sauté pan over medium heat. Add the onions and sauté for 5 minutes. Add the water and half the salt and half the pepper. Cover, reduce the heat to low, and continue cooking, stirring occasionally, until the onions caramelize, 10 to 15 minutes.

Meanwhile, heat the remaining oil over moderate heat in a sauté pan with a 6-inch-diameter bottom. Coarsely shred the potatoes and toss in a bowl with the remaining salt and pepper. Immediately spread the potatoes evenly in the pan, and cook until the bottom is light brown, about 5 minutes. Carefully flip the pancake and cook 2 minutes more.

Transfer the potato pancake, lighter side up, to a baking sheet. Spread its top with the onions. Arrange the olives and rosemary on top.

Preheat the oven to 350 degrees F. Bake for 15 minutes. Transfer to a serving platter and cut into wedges. Serve warm.

HOT TEA AND COCOA

There's something especially warming and comforting about these beverages on a cold weekend morning. Offer your guests a selection of teas, brewed in individual pots. And have your favorite brand of cocoa—and plenty of milk—on hand to whisk up hot and frothy mugfuls as guests request them.

Of course, if anyone insists, you can also offer freshly brewed coffee.

CHAPTER THREE

LUNCH

Wine suggestion:

While the dishes in this menu are fairly light, the strong flavors of the lobster, fennel, and basil—not to mention the garlic of the Caesar Salad—could overwhelm some white wines. So choose a dryish white with some body. A well-balanced Chardonnay, not too oakey or too high in alcohol, such as one from Raymond, Phelps, or Saintsbury is best. Or go for a strong-flavored Fumé Blanc produced by Delorsch, Grgich Hills, or Duckhorn.

Lunch Beside Swan Lake

Serves 4

THE LAKE AND THE FAMILY OF SWANS THAT RESIDE THERE IS THE PERFECT SYMBOL FOR THE Hotel Bel-Air, representing tranquility and a innate sense of style.

This menu features midday favorites with a light and casual touch—perfect fare for lunching beside Swan Lake. There's an inside joke to the menu as well: The hotel kitchen uses only the tender inner leaves of Romaine lettuce for the Caesar Salad, and the outer leaves are part of the swans' regular diet.

At home, serve this lunch on the patio, at a table set up in the garden, or in the sunniest indoor spot. Set the table with floral-patterned china and a bright seasonal bouquet. Various elements of each recipe can be prepared in advance the day before or the morning of the lunch, leaving very little cooking—in particular, boiling the pasta, rapidly sautéing the lobster, and toasting the pound cake—to be done shortly before each course is served.

Seashell Pasta with Lobster, Fennel, Smoked Tomato, and Basil

Caesar Salad with Shaved Parmesan Cheese and Garlic Croutons

Rum Raisin Ice Cream Sandwiches with Toasted Almond Pound Cake
and Caramel Madeira Sauce

SEASHELL PASTA WITH LOBSTER, FENNEL, SMOKED TOMATO, AND BASIL

Though its preparation is fairly simple, one challenge comes in smoking the tomatoes. Yes, you can make it without smoking them, but the pasta won't have the same richness or complexity of flavor. As the instructions below indicate, it isn't difficult to rig up a smoker at home. With the smoking completed well in advance, and the pasta shells preboiled, the rest of the dish's preparation—cooking the lobster with the tomatoes—goes very quickly.

3	large tomatoes, halved and seeded
2	large lobster tails (about ½ pound each), in the shell
20	large pasta shells
½	cup medium pasta shells
½	cup small pasta shells
4	tablespoons olive oil
1	fennel bulb, trimmed and cut crosswise into thin slices
1	tablespoon finely chopped shallots
1	tablespoon finely chopped fresh basil
½	teaspoon salt
¼	teaspoon freshly ground black pepper
2	tablespoons extra virgin olive oil
1½	cups chicken stock
¼	cup white wine
2	medium garlic cloves, finely chopped
1	tablespoon chopped fresh thyme
1	teaspoon salt
¼	teaspoon white pepper
20	basil leaves, torn into large pieces
1	teaspoon champagne vinegar
¼	cup toasted pine nuts
4	small sprigs fresh basil

Smoke the tomatoes in advance. To rig the smoker, light and burn charcoal briquets outdoors in a small barbecue or a large, heavy, beat-up old pot at least 8 inches deep. Soak smoking chips in water until saturated, then drain well. When the coals are nearly exhausted, scatter the soaked chips on top: They should smoulder, giving up smoke without igniting; if they catch fire, spray with a little water from a spray bottle to douse them. When the smoke is heavy, set a fine-mesh rack at least 8 inches above the chips. Place the tomato halves on the rack and cover loosely with a pot lid that will allow some smoke and heat to escape. Smoke for 5 minutes, then remove the tomatoes. When they are cool, cut them into ¼-inch diced pieces and set aside.

Bring a saucepan of water to a boil. Add the lobster tails and blanch for 3 minutes, then drain. Remove the meat from the shells, reserving the shells. Cut the meat in half lengthwise.

Bring a large saucepan of water to a boil, and cook the pasta shells in batches by size until al dente. Drain and set the pasta aside.

In a large skillet, heat 1 tablespoon of olive oil over moderate heat. Add the fennel and shallots and sauté 15 seconds. Remove, season with the salt, pepper, chopped basil, and 1 tablespoon of virgin olive oil, and set aside. In the same pan, heat the remaining olive oil and add the lobster shells, smoked tomatoes, chicken stock, garlic, wine, thyme, salt, and pepper. Simmer 10 to 15 minutes. Discard the lobster shell. Puree the sauce and return to the pan.

Add the lobster meat to the sauce with the basil leaves. Simmer for about 30 seconds; then add the remaining virgin olive oil and the vinegar.

Distribute the sauce with the lobster equally among the serving plates. Separate the large pasta shells and place them on top. Scatter around the small and medium shells. Distribute the fennel among the plates, then garnish with pine nuts and basil.

CAESAR SALAD WITH SHAVED PARMESAN CHEESE AND GARLIC CROUTONS

The classic salad invented by Tijuana chef Caesar Cardini gets a classic preparation and a stylish presentation here. The salad uses only the smaller, tender, inner leaves of Romaine lettuce—those showing a little pale-green-yellow color around their edges. If you bristle against throwing away the larger outer leaves of Romaine—and don't have swans to feed them to—save them for another casual salad.

The dressing, the croutons, and the lettuce leaves may all be prepared several hours in advance, ready to arrange just before serving.

GARLIC CROUTONS

2	tablespoons olive oil
4	medium garlic cloves, finely chopped
1	teaspoon salt
¼	teaspoon white pepper
2 or 3 slices white bread, trimmed of crusts and cut into ½-inch cubes (to yield ¾ cup)

Stir together the oil, garlic, and salt and pepper in a baking pan, and toss the bread cubes in the mixture. Bake at 350 degrees F, turning twice, until golden, about 10 minutes. When the croutons cool, store in an airtight container until serving.

CAESAR DRESSING

3	raw egg yolks, at room temperature
2 or 3 anchovy fillets, finely chopped (about 1 teaspoon)
1	medium garlic clove, finely chopped
2	tablespoons grated Parmesan cheese
1	teaspoon prepared Dijon-style mustard
1	teaspoon red wine vinegar
1	teaspoon salt
½	teaspoon white pepper
½	teaspoon Tabasco sauce
2	tablespoons lemon juice
½	cup extra virgin olive oil

Combine all the ingredients except the lemon juice and olive oil in a food processor with the metal blade, or in a mixing bowl with a wire whisk; blend well. Process or whisk in the lemon juice. Then, beating continuously, add the oil in a slow, thin stream, adding more only as the dressing emulsifies and thickens, until it reaches a thick but still pourable consistency. Cover and refrigerate until serving.

SALAD GREENS

2   heads Romaine lettuce, root ends trimmed off,
     leaves separated, large outer leaves discarded

1   block (¼ pound or larger) Parmesan cheese

Put the Romaine leaves in a large bowl. Add the
Garlic Croutons, 2 tablespoons of freshly grated Parmesan from the block, and enough of the Caesar
Dressing to coat the leaves. Toss thoroughly. Place
the leaves on individual serving plates in a neat stack,
rising largest to smallest leaves. Scatter the croutons
around the stack. With a sharp knife or a cheese
slicer, carefully cut 12 thin shavings—measuring
about 1½ inches by 2½ inches—from the block of
cheese and place these on top of the stacks of leaves.

**Seashell Pasta with Lobster, Fennel, Smoked
Tomato, and Basil**

Rum Raisin Ice Cream Sandwiches with Toasted Almond Pound Cake and Caramel Madeira Sauce

RUM RAISIN ICE CREAM SANDWICHES WITH TOASTED ALMOND POUND CAKE AND CARAMEL MADEIRA SAUCE

In their components and presentation, these are ice cream sandwiches of a very refined sort; yet the overall concept, like more traditional ice cream sandwiches, is very casual indeed. Each element of the dish may be made well in advance, a day ahead of time or more.

You'll have leftovers of pound cake, sauce, and a good deal of ice cream—a good excuse to make a few more sandwiches later on, as well as the Coupe Madeira on page 93.

If you can't find almond meal for the pound cake, you can make your own by finely chopping blanched almond slices in a food processor.

RUM RAISIN ICE CREAM

3	ounces dark rum
¾	cup dark seedless raisins
1	quart milk
½	cup heavy cream
1	cup granulated sugar
1	vanilla bean, split lengthwise
3	whole eggs
5	egg yolks

The night before you make the ice cream, heat the rum in a small saucepan, and pour it over the raisins in a cup or bowl. Cover and refrigerate overnight.

In a saucepan, stir together the milk, cream, half the sugar, and the vanilla bean. Bring to a boil over medium heat.

Meanwhile, whisk the whole eggs and yolks together with the remaining sugar until smooth and light lemon yellow in color. Stir briskly into the boiling milk mixture; then set the bottom of the pan in an ice water bath, stirring frequently, until the mixture cools.

Process in a commercial ice cream maker, following the manufacturer's directions. When the ice cream is almost done but still somewhat soft, stir in the rum and raisins and continue processing until done. Transfer to the freezer.

ALMOND POUND CAKE

½	pound unsalted butter, softened
1	cup granulated sugar
8	whole eggs
	Juice of 2 lemons
	Grated zest of 1 lemon
½	teaspoon almond extract
2	cups almond meal
2	cups all-purpose flour

Preheat the oven to 350 degrees F. In a mixing bowl, cream together the butter and sugar. One at a time, beat in the eggs, then beat in the lemon juice, zest, and almond extract. Sift together the almond meal and flour, and gradually combine them with the creamed mixture to form a smooth batter.

Transfer the batter into a greased 2-quart loaf pan. Bake until golden and a cake tester inserted into the center comes out clean, 45 minutes to 1 hour.

CARAMEL MADEIRA SAUCE

2	cups sugar
1	cup water
	Pinch of cream of tartar
1	cup heavy cream
6	tablespoons Madeira
½	cup dark molasses

Put the sugar, water, and cream of tartar in a deep, heavy, narrow-diameter pan. Stir over low heat until the sugar dissolves completely; then place a candy thermometer in the pan, raise the heat, and boil until the syrup turns light caramel in color, about 330 degrees F on the thermometer.

While the syrup is boiling, combine the cream and Madeira in another pan and warm them over low heat.

As soon as the caramel is ready (330 degrees F), remove it from the heat and dip the bottom of the pan in cold water. Very carefully pour in the cream mixture: It will foam up dramatically. As soon as the foam subsides, stir with a whisk to blend the sauce. Cover and refrigerate until ready to serve.

TOPPINGS

	Confectioner's sugar
2	teaspoons toasted, slivered almonds (for garnish)
4	large strawberries, halved
2	dozen other assorted ripe berries

To make the sandwiches, cut two ½-inch-thick slices of pound cake per portion; with a 3-inch biscuit cutter, cut a circle from each slice. Toast the circles under a preheated broiler until golden brown on both sides.

Drizzle about 2 tablespoons of sauce randomly on each serving plate. Drizzle a contrasting pattern of molasses. At the center of each plate, place a piece of toasted cake and top with a 2-ounce scoop of ice cream. Dust the other pieces of cake with confectioner's sugar, and lean them against the ice cream. Garnish with toasted almonds. Place a few berries alongside each sandwich, and offer extra sauce on the side.

Autumn Beach Picnic at Malibu

Serves 6 to 8

EARLY AUTUMN IN LOS ANGELES IS ONE OF THE MOST WONDERFUL TIMES OF YEAR FOR A PICNIC lunch, with the first hint of coolness in the air—or, perhaps, the heat of a dazzling Indian summer. The harvest time's abundant produce inspires dishes just a touch more robust than might have been appropriate a month or two before.

The fabled Southern California beach community of Malibu, just about a half hour drive from Hotel Bel-Air, provides an ideal setting for such a feast. But the recipes that follow adapt well to any picnic setting, from a backyard table to a tailgate, a favorite park to an apple orchard. All of them may be made as much as a day ahead of time, and they pack well for transporting to the picnic site. If you like, divide up the labor and have various friends prepare different dishes from the menu. Serve right from the containers or, for a more stylish event, carry along an assortment of rustic or elegant platters on which you'll present the food. Be sure to include a lot of the little extras—from cold cuts to fresh fruits to cheeses to breads—that not only really make a picnic but also allow for the inclusion of last-minute guests.

Pasta with Grilled Artichoke Hearts, Roasted Red Bell Peppers, Niçoise Olives, and Grated Romano Cheese

Cucumbers in Yogurt

Roast Chicken Stuffed Under the Skin with Sun-dried Tomatoes and Roasted Garlic

Pico de Gallo

Cannelini Beans with Virgin Olive Oil, Rosemary, and Grilled Fresh Tuna

Hard Salami, Cheeses, Raw Vegetables, Olives, Fresh Fruits, and Crusty Bread

Apple-Cranberry Crumble with Roasted Pecan Streusel

Wine suggestion:

The rustic, casual style of food calls for wines with similar robust freshness. For the white wine, serve a fairly acidic Chardonnay such as Sonoma Cutrer "Russian River," Simi, or Navarro. A slightly chilled red wine with good body and acidity, such as Chateauneuf-du-Pape or Gigondas from France would be appropriate, as would Dolcetto, a Beaujolais-style red from the Piedmont in Italy. Also bear in mind when eating the pasta dish that artichokes have a tendency to make most wines taste a little bit strange, and it may take a few sips afterward—or a sip or two of water—until your palate readjusts.

PASTA WITH GRILLED ARTICHOKE HEARTS, ROASTED RED BELL PEPPERS, NIÇOISE OLIVES, AND GRATED ROMANO CHEESE

Though this recipe includes lots of ingredients, the preparation is really fairly simple, and all of the elements combine into a wonderfully colorful and harmonious salad. Prepare and package the artichokes and the pasta mixture separately, combining them as directed when you reach your picnic destination.

	Juice of ½ lemon
8	*medium artichokes*
1	*cup haricots verts (French-style green beans), cut on the bias into 1-inch pieces*
½	*cup yellow wax beans, cut on the bias into 1-inch pieces*
¼	*cup olive oil*
2	*medium garlic cloves, finely chopped*
1	*tablespoon finely chopped shallots*
1	*tablespoon salt*
1	*teaspoon white pepper*
½	*cup white wine*
1	*cup chicken stock*
2	*tablespoons lemon juice*
1	*tablespoon chopped fresh thyme*
	Grated zest of 2 lemons
½	*cup green Niçoise olives, pitted*
3	*medium red bell peppers, roasted, peeled, seeded, and julienned*
5	*tablespoons extra virgin olive oil*
3	*cups linguini, cooked al dente*
⅔	*cup coarsely grated Pecorino Romano cheese*
1	*tablespoon chopped fresh sage leaves*
	Salt to taste
	Freshly ground black pepper to taste

Fill a bowl with cold water, and squeeze the lemon into it.

To prepare each artichoke, snap off its leaves, starting at the stem end and working upward in circles until you reach the top third or so. Cut off this portion of leaves to reveal the fuzzy choke; scoop it out with a sharp-edged spoon and discard. Pare away the artichoke's tough outer skin with a small, sharp knife. Cut the remaining artichoke bottom into 8 wedges, and put them in the bowl of water.

Bring water to a boil in a medium saucepan, and blanch the beans for 2 minutes. Drain and spread them out on a plate or tray to cool. Set aside.

In a large skillet, heat the olive oil over high heat. Drain the artichokes well, patting them dry, and add them to the skillet; sauté 2 minutes. Stir in the garlic, shallots, salt, and pepper, then add the white wine and continue cooking until the liquid evaporates. Add the chicken stock and lemon juice and cook until they evaporate. Test a piece of artichoke to see if it is tender-crisp; if not, add ½ cup of water and cook until evaporated, then test again. Add the thyme and lemon zests and cook 1 minute more. Remove from the heat, and let the artichokes cool.

Preheat a barbecue, gas grill, or broiler. Place the artichokes on a fine-mesh screen for the barbecue or grill, or on the broiler tray. Grill or broil until golden brown, turning once, about 5 minutes.

While the artichokes are still warm, toss them in a mixing bowl with all of the olives, half the peppers, and 2 tablespoons of the virgin olive oil.

In a separate bowl, toss the pasta with the remaining oil and peppers, the beans, half the cheese, and the sage. Season with salt and pepper.

To serve, arrange the pasta mixture in the center of a large serving platter. Scatter the cooled artichoke mixture around the pasta; sprinkle the artichokes with the remaining cheese.

CUCUMBERS IN YOGURT

There is really no need for a recipe for this classic combination. Just slice up cucumbers thinly or thickly as you like, peeling them first if their peels are thick and bitter, and halving and seeding them first if they are large and have prominent seeds. Then just toss with enough plain yogurt to coat the slices well, season to taste with salt and pepper, and add some fresh herbs if you like, such as Italian parsley or a little mint. Chill well, and carry to the picnic in a sealed container.

ROAST CHICKEN STUFFED UNDER THE SKIN WITH SUN-DRIED TOMATOES AND ROASTED GARLIC

You can roast these fragrant chickens the day before the picnic, refrigerating them after they cool. Carry them whole to the picnic site, to be cut or carved into pieces or slices once you get there.

2	*whole heads garlic*
3	*tablespoons olive oil*
¼	*cup sun-dried tomatoes, finely chopped*
3	*tablespoons finely chopped rosemary leaves*
3	*tablespoons finely chopped sage leaves*
2	*4½- to 5-pound free-range chickens*
	Salt to taste
	Freshly ground black pepper to taste

Preheat the oven to 350 degrees F. Cut about ½ inch off the top of each head of garlic. Place them on a large sheet of heavy-duty aluminum foil, and drizzle with 1 tablespoon of the oil. Seal the foil tightly around them and roast until the cloves are tender, 30 to 35 minutes. When the garlic is cool enough to handle, squeeze the pulp out of each clove into a mixing bowl, and mash together with the sun-dried tomatoes, rosemary, and sage.

Carefully inserting your fingers between the skin and flesh of each chicken, gently separate and loosen the skin over the entire breast. With your fingers, spread the garlic mixture evenly between the skin and breast meat on both chickens.

Rub 1 tablespoon of olive oil evenly over the entire surface of each chicken. Thoroughly season both chickens, inside and out, with salt and pepper. Put the chickens in a roasting pan, breasts up, and roast until the juices run clear when a thin skewer is inserted into the thickest part of the thigh, about 1¼ hours. Serve warm or cold.

A picnic at Malibu is the perfect setting for such foods as Cannelini Beans with Virgin Olive Oil and Pasta with Grilled Artichoke Hearts.

Vegetables packed in olive oil are delicious picnic foods that transport easily.

PICO DE GALLO

"Rooster's beak" in Spanish refers to a variety of different piquant salads and salsas, including this lively combination of citrus fruits, red onions, bell peppers, fresh herbs, and dried chili. It makes a spectacular companion to the roast chicken.

Prepare all the ingredients a day in advance; that includes the easy though time-consuming task of peeling the membranes from the citrus segments, which gives the salad a finer color and texture. Then refrigerate all the fruits and vegetables individually in covered containers or plastic bags. Transport them in their containers to the picnic site, tossing them all together with the seasonings at the last minute for the freshest-tasting results.

½   cup thinly sliced red onion

1   cup orange segments (or a combination of orange and tangerine, clementine, or mandarin)

½   cup grapefruit segments

¼   cup julienned red bell peppers

¼   cup julienned green bell peppers

¼   cup lime segments

¼   cup extra virgin olive oil

1   tablespoon chopped fresh mint leaves

1   teaspoon chopped fresh cilantro leaves

1   teaspoon red chili flakes

1   teaspoon finely cracked black pepper

½   teaspoon chopped fresh thyme

Fresh mint sprigs (for garnish)

Assemble all the ingredients in advance, chilling the fruits and vegetables well in the refrigerator. Just before serving, toss everything together thoroughly with the seasonings in a mixing bowl. Garnish with mint sprigs.

CANNELINI BEANS WITH VIRGIN OLIVE OIL, ROSEMARY, AND GRILLED FRESH TUNA

Easily prepared well in advance, this version of a favorite Italian antipasto makes an excellent picnic dish. You can start marinating the tuna up to a day ahead, and cook the beans either the day before or the morning of the picnic (allowing, of course, for overnight soaking before you cook them). The prosciutto trimmings called for here should cost much less than regular sliced prosciutto, so be sure to ask your butcher if they're available.

If there's a barbecue at the picnic site, carry the tuna there raw in its marinade, to be grilled just before serving. Alternatively, grill or broil the tuna before you leave home, and serve it lukewarm or cold.

CANNELINI BEANS

2   cups dried cannelini beans

6   tablespoons olive oil

½   fennel bulb, cut into 4 pieces

½   medium white onion, cut into 4 pieces

2   medium garlic cloves, finely chopped

½   teaspoon red chili flakes

1½   tablespoons salt

6   cups chicken broth

2   ounces prosciutto ham trimmings

10   cracked black peppercorns

2   bay leaves

2   sprigs fresh thyme

½   cup extra virgin olive oil

25   small fresh basil leaves

Salt to taste

Freshly ground black pepper to taste

Begin by putting the beans in a mixing bowl, covering well with cold water, and soaking overnight.

The next day, heat the olive oil in a 1-gallon stockpot over moderate heat. Add the fennel and onion and sauté 2 minutes; then add the garlic and chili and sauté 2 minutes more, stirring constantly. Add the salt and sauté 1 minute more. Add the broth. Tie the ham, peppercorns, bay leaves, and thyme in a piece of cheesecloth, and add it to the pot. Bring to a boil, reduce the heat, and simmer for 15 minutes.

Drain the beans of their soaking liquid, and add them to the pot. Simmer until done al dente, about 45 minutes, adding water to the pot as needed to keep the beans submerged; take care not to mush the beans. Then strain off the cooking liquid, reserving it as a soup base.

While the beans are still warm, toss them with the virgin olive oil until it is absorbed. Then toss in the basil leaves and season with salt and pepper.

GRILLED FRESH TUNA

1¼ *pounds fresh tuna fillet, cut into steaks ¾-inch thick, then trimmed into 12 to 14 triangular pieces*

Grated zest of 2 lemons

1 *small garlic clove, finely chopped*

1 *tablespoon freshly ground black pepper*

½ *tablespoon salt*

1 *tablespoon chopped fresh parsley*

½ *tablespoon chopped fresh thyme*

3 *tablespoons olive oil*

Fresh basil sprigs (for garnish)

Begin marinating the tuna as early as 24 hours before serving or as little as 3 hours ahead. Season the pieces all over with the lemon zest, garlic, pepper, salt, parsley, and thyme, then drizzle with olive oil. Refrigerate in a covered dish.

Preheat the grill or broiler until very hot. Then cook the tuna until it is well seared on the outside but still very pink in the center, about 45 seconds per side; the tuna will go on cooking after you remove it from the grill, winding up a little pink inside.

To serve, spread the beans on a large platter. Arrange the tuna pieces on top and garnish with basil sprigs.

HARD SALAMI, CHEESES, RAW VEGETABLES, OLIVES, FRESH FRUIT, AND CRUSTY BREAD

These are the little extras that turn a great picnic into a memorable feast—casual foods that, like a still-life, decorate the picnic table and invite guests to nibble. There is no specific plan to follow in what you buy: Just plan a foray to your best-stocked gourmet market or deli the day before the picnic, and purchase fairly generous quantities of various easily transported savory and sweet items to lend extra variety to the meal.

APPLE-CRANBERRY CRUMBLE WITH ROASTED PECAN STREUSEL

Bake this heartwarming autumnal dessert an hour or two before leaving for the picnic. Then wrap it well in aluminum foil and kitchen towels, so you can dish it up still slightly warm at the end of the feast.

If you like, bring along a carton or two of fresh cream to drizzle over individual servings.

ROASTED PECAN STREUSEL

½ *pound shelled pecans*

12 *tablespoons unsalted butter, softened*

¾ *cup brown sugar*

2 *cups all-purpose flour*

1½ *ounces almond paste*

1 *teaspoon ground cinnamon*

½ *teaspoon ground mace*

Spread the pecans on a baking sheet, and roast them in a 325 degree F oven for 8 minutes. Allow to cool thoroughly, then put the nuts in a food processor with the metal blade, and pulse until finely chopped. Then remove half the nuts and add 4 tablespoons of the butter; continue processing until the nuts form a smooth paste.

In a mixing bowl, use your fingers to rub the paste together with the chopped pecans and all the remaining ingredients until they form a crumbly mixture. Set aside.

APPLE-CRANBERRY FILLING

1¼ *cups sugar*

1 *cup orange juice*

Grated zest of 1 orange

¾ *pound whole cranberries*

4 *large cooking apples, Macintosh or other*

2 *tablespoons unsalted butter*

2 *tablespoons maple syrup*

2 *tablespoons honey*

2 *tablespoons Calvados*

2 *cups heavy cream (optional)*

Put 1 cup of the sugar, along with the orange juice and zest, in a medium saucepan; bring to a boil, stirring frequently, over moderate heat and simmer for 10 minutes. Add the cranberries and simmer 5 minutes more. Remove from the heat and let cool.

Peel, core, and cut the apples into ½-inch-thick slices. In a separate saucepan, melt the butter over moderate heat and add the apples, the remaining sugar, the syrup, and honey. Cook the apples until they are soft but not mushy, about 5 minutes. Remove from the heat and stir in the Calvados.

To assemble and cook the crumble, preheat the oven to 400 degrees F. Stir together the apple and cranberry mixtures and put them in a buttered 2½-quart baking dish. Crumble the streusel mixture over the surface. Bake until bubbly and golden, about 20 minutes. Serve hot or lukewarm, scooped into bowls. Drizzle with cream, if you like.

Wine suggestion:

The slightly astringent taste of the oysters requires a white that is fairly neutral, such as a Muscadet, or an austere style of California Fumé Blanc like those from Deloach or Mondavi. The pork calls for a medium-bodied Pinot Noir such as Mondavi "unfiltered," Saintsbury "Carneros," Wild Horse, Barrow & Green, or La Crema.

POOLSIDE COOKOUT
Serves 10 to 12

THE QUIET CHARM OF THE BEL-AIR'S SWIMMING POOL LENDS ITSELF ESPECIALLY WELL TO CASUAL summertime entertaining. Come September, it's the perfect spot for a late-summer cookout featuring more adventurous but no-less-casual foods that hint of the autumn soon to come.

This menu is ideal for your own home cookout—come Labor Day, or anytime the weather beckons you outdoors. As a matter of fact, you don't even need to have a patio or backyard; all the recipes adapt well to cooking indoors, with a stovetop grill or broiler and an oven rotisserie.

BARBECUED SHOULDER OF PORK WITH VINEGAR MOP

CORN ROASTED IN THE HUSK

ROAST OYSTERS WITH SHALLOT-BROWN BUTTER VINAIGRETTE

GRILLED VEGETABLE PLATTER WITH FRESH HERBS

COBB SALAD

SAGE HONEY ICE CREAM WITH FRESH FIGS, APRICOTS, AND PLUMS

BARBECUED SHOULDER OF PORK WITH VINEGAR MOP

"Mop" is an old Southern term for a barbecue baste, mopped onto the meat during cooking with a basting brush or a piece of cloth on a stick.

The best way to cook the meat is on a barbecue rotisserie. Alternatively, you can place the meat directly on the grill well away from the heat; keep the heat low and the cover closed, and turn the meat often. The meat may also be cooked a day in advance and pulled into pieces, to be moistened with a little of the marinade and reheated in the oven.

2   *tablespoons salt*

1   *tablespoon freshly ground black pepper*

1   *tablespoon Hungarian paprika*

1   *tablespoon ground coriander*

2   *teaspoons ground cumin*

1   *teaspoon ground cinnamon*

2   *garlic cloves, finely chopped*

8   *pounds whole boneless pork shoulder*

In a small bowl, stir together the salt, pepper, paprika, coriander, cumin, cinnamon, and garlic. Rub the mixture all over the pork shoulder, working it well into the meat. Roll up the shoulder and tie securely with kitchen string.

Preheat a barbecue with rotisserie and hood. When the coals turn white, soak 2 large handfuls of smoking chips in cold water. Drain well and spread the chips on the coals. Skewer pork shoulder on the rotisserie spit and, as soon as smoke develops from the chips, set the meat turning above the coals and lower the hood, leaving the vents completely open. Lift the hood after the smoke dissipates, about 20 minutes or so.

Roast Oysters with Shallot-Brown Butter Vinaigrette. Corn Roasted in the Husk. Grilled Vegetables with Fresh Herbs.

VINEGAR MOP

1½   *cups vegetable oil*

¾   *cup apple cider vinegar*

¼   *cup spicy mustard*

¼   *cup tomato ketchup*

Prepare the vinegar mop by stirring together the oil, vinegar, mustard, and ketchup. Heat briefly in a saucepan.

Baste the shoulder with the vinegar mop every 20 minutes while it cooks. Continue cooking and basting until the meat is done and very tender, 3½ to 4 hours.

To serve, cut the strings and, with forks, pull the meat apart into chunks and shreds, moistening it with any remaining mop.

CORN ROASTED IN THE HUSK

If you're barbecuing, this is the easiest way imaginable to cook corn: You don't even have to husk or string it first, since the husks and silk peel off easily once they are charred. Serve the corn with melted butter, salt, and pepper.

If you have access to the corn at its source, try to buy the ears with good lengths of stalk still attached, since the stalks make convenient handles for eating the corn. The quantities below assume that some people will want seconds. Adjust the amount according to your knowledge of your own guests' appetites.

18   *ears fresh sweet corn, husks and silk left on*

    Unsalted butter to taste

    Salt to taste

    Freshly ground black pepper to taste

With a serrated bread knife, cut about 1 inch from the end of each ear, exposing a narrow cross-section of cob.

Preheat the barbecue or grill to moderate to high, or preheat the oven to 375 degrees F. Place the ears of corn on the grill and cook, turning often, until their husks turn evenly dark brown, 10 to 15 minutes; in the oven, place the ears on the rack and roast, turning once, for about 20 minutes.

Serve the corn in the husks, leaving guests to peel them back (the strings come away with them) and season with butter, salt, and pepper.

ROAST OYSTERS WITH SHALLOT-BROWN BUTTER VINAIGRETTE

It's an easy task to roast fresh oysters on top of the barbecue. Alternatively, you can cook them in the oven. The warm vinaigrette, prepared while the oysters cook, adds just the right touch of piquancy and richness.

36   *fresh oysters in their shells, unopened*

SHALLOT-BROWN BUTTER VINAIGRETTE

1   *pound unsalted butter*

½   *cup finely chopped fresh shallots*

1   *tablespoon walnut oil*

1   *small garlic clove, finely chopped*

¼   *cup red wine vinegar*

¼   *cup liquid drained from pickled capers*

2   *tablespoons freshly ground black pepper*

1   *tablespoon lemon juice*

    Grated zest of 2 lemons

Preheat the barbecue or grill until very hot; or preheat the oven to 375 degrees F.

Scrub the oyster shells clean, using as little water as necessary to rinse. Stack the oysters, 2 or 3 deep on a sheet pan, and cover loosely with aluminum foil. Place the pan on the hot grill or in the oven and roast just until their shells pop open, 7 to 10 minutes.

The instant the oysters start cooking, prepare the vinaigrette. Melt the butter in a medium saucepan over low to moderate heat. Continue heating until the milk solids separate to the bottom and the clear butter on top begins to develop a light brown color. Remove from the heat and let it sit for a minute or two, then carefully pour the clear liquid into a bowl, leaving all the sediment behind. Add the shallots, walnut oil, and garlic to the clarified butter, leaving them to steep a few minutes. Just before serving, add the remaining ingredients and whisk thoroughly to blend.

Serve the oysters from their tray or a platter, with the vinaigrette on the side for guests to spoon on the oysters as they wish.

GRILLED VEGETABLE PLATTER WITH FRESH HERBS

Briefly marinated with a mixture of olive oil and fresh herbs and then grilled, this array of fresh vegetables makes a beautiful and delicious companion to barbecued meats. You can cook it just before guests arrive and serve it hot; or prepare it ahead of time, serving the vegetables cold.

Any dense-textured vegetable will grill well, though different vegetables will require slight variations of preparation as outlined below. Select 2 or more vegetables for your tray, opting for whatever is in peak condition at the market.

2½ to 3 pounds fresh vegetables (zucchini, yellow squash, patty pan squash, Japanese eggplant, new potatoes, sweet potatoes, baby carrots, shiitake mushrooms, red onions, bulb fennel, asparagus)

½   cup extra virgin olive oil

2   tablespoons finely chopped shallots

1   tablespoon finely chopped fresh rosemary

1   tablespoon finely chopped fresh thyme

1   tablespoon finely chopped fresh mint

1   tablespoon grated Parmesan cheese

1   tablespoon salt

2   teaspoons freshly ground black pepper

3   tablespoons balsamic vinegar

¼   cup toasted pine nuts

Cut zucchini, squash, and eggplant on the bias into ½-inch-thick slices. Cut new potatoes in half. Cut sweet potatoes into ¼-inch-thick slices and blanch in boiling water for 1 minute. Blanch baby carrots whole for 1 minute. Stem the mushrooms, leaving the caps whole. Cut the onions crosswise into ⅓-inch-thick slices, separating them into rings. Cut the fennel into ½-inch-thick wedges. Trim the asparagus stems.

Preheat the barbecue. Cover part of the grill with a metal screen on which to grill the smaller items.

In a large mixing bowl, stir together the oil, shallots, and herbs. Toss the vegetables—with the exception of eggplant and mushrooms—with the oil mixture; lightly brush the eggplant and mushrooms separately with a little of the oil. Add the Parmesan, salt, and pepper to the vegetables and toss well; then toss in the eggplant and mushrooms.

Grill the vegetables until each is golden brown on both sides, 5 to 7 minutes total. Remove each vegetable as it is done and transfer to a serving platter, arranging them in an attractive pattern. When all the vegetables are done, sprinkle with the balsamic vinegar and pine nuts. Serve hot or cold.

COBB SALAD

The Bel-Air presents a classic version of this favorite lunchtime salad, which makes a colorful and fresh-tasting addition to the cookout table.

Much of the preparation can be done an hour or two in advance: mixing the dressing, cooking and dicing the bacon, grilling the chicken breasts, crumbling the cheese, chopping the tomatoes. But hold off on peeling and dicing the avocado until the last minute, so that it doesn't discolor; and chop the lettuce at the same time, to preserve its crisp, fresh texture.

SALAD

2   heads Romaine lettuce, large outer leaves discarded

   Salt to taste

   Freshly ground black pepper to taste

3   ripe Haas avocados, halved, peeled, pitted, and diced into ½-inch pieces

2   pounds boned and skinned chicken breasts, seasoned with salt and pepper, grilled or broiled, and diced into ½-inch pieces

3   vine-ripened tomatoes, halved, seeded, and diced into ¼-inch pieces

1   cup crumbled blue cheese

10   thick slices bacon, cooked crisp and diced into ¼-inch pieces

Chop the Romaine leaves into ½-inch pieces. Season with salt and pepper and spread in the bottom of a large, wide serving bowl.

Arrange the avocado in a vertical strip across the center of the lettuce. On one side of the avocado, arrange the chicken pieces in another strip; on the other side, arrange the tomato. Next to the chicken, arrange the bacon; next to the tomato, the blue cheese.

LEMON VINAIGRETTE

¾   cup olive oil

   Juice and grated zest of 2 lemons

1   teaspoon finely chopped shallots

1   teaspoon chopped fresh thyme

1   teaspoon chopped fresh Italian parsley

1   teaspoon salt

½   teaspoon finely chopped garlic

¼   teaspoon freshly ground black pepper

Stir together all the ingredients. When ready to serve, present the salad at the table and pour about two-thirds of the dressing over it. Toss well and serve, passing additional dressing on the side.

SAGE HONEY ICE CREAM WITH FRESH FIGS, APRICOTS, AND PLUMS

The aromatic sweetness of honey derived from sage blossoms gives a distinctive flavor to this rich ice cream, which is wonderfully complemented by an array of fresh summer fruits.

The quantities below yield about 1 gallon of ice cream.

2   quarts milk

1   quart heavy cream

2½   cups sage honey, at warm room temperature

16   egg yolks

In a saucepan, stir together the milk, cream, and half the honey. Bring to a boil over medium heat. Meanwhile, gradually whisk the remaining honey into the egg yolks until smooth. Stir briskly into the boiling milk mixture; then set the bottom of the pan in an ice water bath, stirring frequently, until the mixture cools.

Process in a commercial ice cream maker, following the manufacturer's directions. Transfer to the freezer.

Serve with a bowl of fresh ripe summer fruit.

The Hotel Bel-Air's swimming pool is the perfect spot for a cookout.

Fireside Lunch for a Blustery Day
Serves 6

ONE OF HOTEL BEL-AIR'S NUMEROUS FIRESIDES—WHETHER INDOORS IN THE BAR OR A PRIVATE SUITE, or outdoors at one of several open-air hearths on the hotel grounds—is a perfect setting for this casual, heartwarming lunch.

The menu is equally perfect for an autumn or winter weekend lunch at home. The bean soup may be prepared well ahead of time, as may the maple ice cream. The sweet potato fritters require minimal work. And the sandwiches, though a fairly long recipe, are straightforward and simple work; the spectacular-tasting results more than justify the time.

Serve the meal at a table set by your own fireside. Or present it in the kitchen or the dining room, where you've lit candles whose glow will brighten an overcast day.

Wine suggestion:

Both the soup and the sandwiches will go well with a fruity Merlot, such as those from Shafer or Clos du Bois.

SEVEN-BEAN SOUP WITH FRIED LEEKS

PETITE SANDWICHES OF ROAST VEAL AND GRILLED ZUCCHINI ON CARAWAY ONION ROLLS, WITH BABY BEETS AND NEW POTATOES

CINNAMON-DUSTED SWEET POTATO FRITTERS WITH MAPLE ICE CREAM

CHAPTER FOUR

TEATIME

A Courtyard Tea Tasting

Serves 10 to 12

T EATIME HAS BECOME A DELIGHTFULLY CIVILIZED OCCASION WORLDWIDE. AT THE BEL-AIR, THE moment is marked not merely in the traditional English way—with pots of tea accompanied by dainty sandwiches and pastries—but with a more far-reaching, cosmopolitan approach that also embraces Southern California's close ties to the Pacific Rim. The tea service here offers a wide range of tasting options: in the teas themselves and in the sweet and savory bites that accompany them.

At home, this tasting menu offers even more options: For a large gathering, you can offer all the dishes; for smaller get-togethers, make fewer recipes, selecting those that appeal to you most and are most appropriate to the occasion. Do offer, though, at least 3 different teas, served from individual pots for each guest or several larger pots. And set out a stack of small dishes, forks, and napkins, allowing your guests to serve themselves from platters of the tea foods you've prepared. In warm weather, present the tea in the sunniest spot available; when the weather grows colder, the fireside is an appropriate setting.

ARRAY OF TEAS

TOMATO-AND-BASIL SANDWICHES ON CORN BREAD

SNOWPEA-CASHEW-FRIED RICE SPRING ROLLS

PECAN CARAMEL TARTLETS

BANANA-FIG TOAST WITH TANGERINE CREAM CHEESE

COCONUT SHORTBREADS

SESAME CHICKEN SKEWERS WITH ORANGE-GINGER GLAZE

SMOKED-SALMON-AND-CUCUMBER SANDWICHES ON ONION BREAD

DRY SHERRY

ARRAY OF TEAS

Depending on the number of guests, offer a choice of 3 or more different teas. While dozens of different teas exist, begin your explorations of tea by selecting contrasting examples from the following outstanding and popular varieties:

GREEN TEAS: Teas that are processed and dried without fermenting, producing a fine, pale, fresh green-tasting beverage, best enjoyed without milk.

Chun Mee. A fine Chinese tea with a crisp, dry taste and fresh aroma.

Dragon Well. A rare Chinese tea with remarkable clarity and a rich yet delicate flavor.

Gunpowder. Subtle, sweet, and pungent. The name comes from the small pellet shapes into which the leaves of this Chinese tea are rolled.

Gyokuru. Japan's finest tea, sweet and delicate yet higher in caffeine than most teas.

Yunnan Tipped. A fine-tasting tea made from small young bud leaves.

OOLONG TEAS: Partly fermented teas, somewhat stronger and darker than greens, enjoyed plain, with lemon or with milk.

Formosa. From Taiwan, an outstanding tea that yields an aromatic brew at once both pungent and fruity.

Mainland. From mainland China, a brisk, rich-tasting cup.

BLACK TEAS: Fully fermented teas that yield a rich, strong, dark, and aromatic brew, best appreciated with milk or lemon.

Assam. From India, a high-quality, full-bodied, pungent and malty brew.

Ceylon. From Sri Lanka, a somewhat softer tea exhibiting qualities similar to Assam.

Darjeeling. Grown on Himalayan slopes in northeast India, this renowned tea produces a deep reddish brown liquor with full-bodied, rich flavor.

Keemun. From northern China, a full-flavored, thick-bodied tea.

Lapsang Souchong. Produced in India, China, and Indonesia, this tea is renowned for its richly aromatic smoky flavor.

BLENDS: Teas blended from two or more different varieties of leaves.

English Breakfast. A traditional, eye-opening blend of Keemun and other black teas from India and Sri Lanka. Excellent both in the morning and at teatime, with milk and sugar.

Irish Breakfast. A robust blend of Assam and Ceylon black teas, served with milk and sugar.

Earl Grey. A blend of black teas delightfully scented with the oil of the rare citrus fruit known as bergamot. Very popular at teatime.

To brew the tea, start with fresh, cold water, brought to a full boil; do not reboil water that has already boiled once, as it will produce a flat-tasting cup. Heat one or more teapots by filling them with an inch or two of boiling water, then swirl it and pour it out. Measure 1 rounded teaspoon of tea leaves per cup into each pot, adding an extra spoonful for pots holding 6 or more cups; put the tea in an infusion ball large enough to allow for its expansion, or add it loose to the pot if you have tea strainers to pour it through. Pour in boiling water and steep for 3 minutes, then pour.

Offer pitchers of milk, a sugar bowl, and a plate of thinly sliced lemon for guests to add to their cups of tea as they wish.

TOMATO-AND-BASIL SANDWICHES ON CORN BREAD

An English teatime favorite gets a fresh, contemporary twist with the addition of fresh basil leaves and a flavorful yeast bread enriched by cornmeal and fresh corn. Instead of baking the bread, you can substitute an egg-enriched or multigrain loaf.

CORN BREAD

1   packet active dried yeast

½   cup warm water

3½   cups bread flour

½   cup masa harina (Mexican-style cornmeal)

2   teaspoons salt

½   cup pureed sweetcorn kernels (fresh or canned)

2   tablespoons vegetable oil

Stir the yeast into the water, and leave at room temperature about 10 minutes to activate.

Combine the flour, onion, chives, and salt in an electric mixer with the dough hook (or by hand, see page 30). With the mixer running on its slowest speed, pour the yeast and remaining ingredients into the flour mixture, and knead the dough until smooth and elastic, about 10 minutes.

Cover the bowl securely with plastic wrap, and leave it at warm room temperature until doubled in bulk, about 1½ hours. Punch the dough down, empty onto a floured work surface, and shape it into an oblong loaf. Place in a greased 2-quart loaf pan, cover loosely with a kitchen towel, and let rise at room temperature until doubled in bulk, about 1 hour.

Place a baking pan on the oven floor, and preheat the oven to 400 degrees F. Put the risen loaf in the oven and, being extremely careful to avoid the steam, immediately pour ½ cup of water into the baking pan at the bottom of the oven.

Bake the bread until it is well risen and golden and sounds hollow when rapped with a knuckle, about 40 minutes. Do not open the oven door during the first 20 minutes of baking. Cool to room temperature on a wire rack before slicing.

TOMATO-AND-BASIL FILLING

¾   cup mascarpone

¾   pound Roma tomatoes, thinly sliced

¾   cup tightly packed, finely shredded fresh basil leaves

To make the sandwiches, cut 6 lengthwise slices, ¼ inch thick, from the loaf of bread. Thinly spread one side of each slice with mascarpone. Place the tomato slices in a single layer on 3 of the slices. Thinly spread the mascarpone over tomatoes. Sprinkle the basil leaves evenly on top. Cover with the remaining bread slices. With a sharp knife, cut the sandwiches into a variety of small shapes and arrange on a serving platter.

SNOWPEA-CASHEW-FRIED RICE SPRING ROLLS

Light in taste and texture, these vegetarian spring rolls are easily prepared and partly cooked in advance, to be popped in hot oil and crisped to a golden brown just before serving.

FRIED RICE

3   tablespoons peanut oil

1½   cups cooked white rice

3   tablespoons chopped scallions

1   tablespoon sesame seeds

1   tablespoon soy sauce

Heat the oil in a medium skillet over high heat. Add the cooked rice, scallions, and sesame seeds. Stir-fry for 1 minute; then stir in the soy sauce, remove from the heat, and cool to room temperature.

FILLING AND SPRING ROLLS

¼   cup peanut oil

2   cups snow peas, julienned

½   cup carrots, julienned

½   cup celery, julienned

½   cup thinly sliced onions

1½   cups thinly sliced Nappa cabbage

1   cup cashews, roasted in a 350 degree F oven for 10 minutes, then finely chopped

1   teaspoon finely grated lemon zest

1   teaspoon finely grated lime zest

¾   teaspoon chili flakes

¾   teaspoon salt

¼   teaspoon freshly ground black pepper

     Cornstarch (for dusting)

20   egg roll wrappers

2   eggs, lightly beaten

Heat the oil in a large skillet over high heat. Add the snow peas, carrots, celery, and onion, and stir-fry for about 30 seconds. Add the Fried Rice, cabbage, cashews, lemon and lime zests, chili flakes, salt, and pepper; remove from the heat and stir well. Set aside to cool to room temperature.

On a work surface lightly dusted with cornstarch, place an egg roll wrapper with one corner pointing toward you, like a diamond. Lightly brush its edges with beaten egg. Place 4 tablespoons of the filling in the center of the wrapper. Fold the corner nearest you over the filling; fold in the 2 side corners, then roll up the spring roll away from you to form a cylinder with the tip of the topmost corner showing at its middle. Lightly dust the egg roll with cornstarch. Repeat with the remaining wrappers and filling.

To prefry the spring rolls, heat 2 quarts of vegetable oil in a heavy 3-quart pot or deep fryer to 275 degrees F on a deep-frying thermometer. Cook the spring rolls in several batches, without crowding, until very pale golden, about 3 minutes; transfer to paper towels to drain and hold until serving time. Before serving, heat the oil to 350 degrees F and fry 1 to 2 minutes or until golden; drain on paper towels and serve immediately.

To cook the spring rolls completely once they have been shaped, deep-fry in oil that is 350 degrees F until golden brown, about 3 minutes. Drain on paper towels and serve immediately.

PECAN CARAMEL TARTLETS

No tea array would be complete without at least one wonderful bite-size pastry, and these rich and nutty little tarts fit the bill perfectly.

Though the idea of pastry making may seem daunting, these are very easy to prepare. The caramel can be made as much as a week in advance and refrigerated in a covered container; gently reheat it before assembling the tartlets. (The quantities given yield about 1 cup of caramel; save the leftover sauce for ice cream sundaes.) And you can mix the shortcrust dough several days ahead of time, and shape and bake it the day before you fill and serve the pastries.

CARAMEL

¾   cup sugar

½   cup water

     Pinch of cream of tartar

¼   cup heavy cream

2   tablespoons unsalted butter

Put the sugar, water, and cream of tartar in a deep, heavy, narrow-diameter pan. Stir over low heat until the sugar dissolves completely. Place a candy thermometer in the pan, raise the heat, and boil until the syrup turns light caramel in color, about 330 degrees F on the thermometer.

While the syrup is boiling, put the cream in another pan and warm over low heat.

As soon as the caramel is ready, remove it from the heat and dip the bottom of the pan in cold water. Very carefully pour in the cream: It will foam up dramatically. As soon as the foam subsides, stir in the butter with a whisk to blend.

SHORTCRUST DOUGH

10   tablespoons unsalted butter

¼   cup plus 1 teaspoon sugar

1   egg

1   cup cake flour

     Pinch of salt

     Grated zest of 1 lemon

Cream together the butter and sugar. Beat in the egg. Stir together the remaining ingredients, and then stir into the creamed mixture just until they form a dough. Gather into a ball, wrap in plastic wrap, and refrigerate for at least 1 hour or until ready to use.

Preheat the oven to 350 degrees F. On a lightly floured surface, roll out the dough to a ⅛-inch thickness. Cut into rounds with a 2½-inch-diameter biscuit cutter. Lightly flour 2-inch tartlet molds and line them with the rounds of dough. Bake until light golden, 10 to 15 minutes. Unmold the shells and cool to room temperature.

PECAN FILLING

1½   cups broken pecan pieces

¼   cup dark seedless raisins

½   cup powdered sugar

To assemble the tartlets, stir together the pecans and raisins with ½ cup of the caramel. Thoroughly dust the pastry shells with powdered sugar. Place 3 tablespoons of the pecan mixture into each shell.

BANANA-FIG TOAST WITH TANGERINE CREAM CHEESE

Pound cake, a frequent accompaniment to tea, is dressed up in this recipe with fresh banana and dried figs, then toasted and spread with a zesty whipped cream cheese. Both the cake and its spread can be made a day ahead of time.

BANANA-FIG POUND CAKE

7   *ounces unsalted butter, softened*

½   *cup sugar*

5   *very ripe bananas*

¾   *cup dark rum*

3   *eggs*

1½   *cups all-purpose flour*

1   *cup finely chopped dried figs*

1   *cup finely chopped pecans*

1   *tablespoon baking powder*

¾   *teaspoon ground ginger*

¾   *teaspoon grated nutmeg*

Preheat the oven to 325 degrees F. Cream together the butter, sugar, and bananas until smooth. Stir in the rum, then beat in the eggs one at a time.

Toss ¼ cup of the flour with the figs and pecans. Combine the remaining flour with the baking powder, ginger, and nutmeg. Gradually stir the dry ingredients into the creamed mixture. Finally, fold in the figs and pecans.

Transfer the batter to a greased 2-quart loaf pan. Bake until golden and a cake tester inserted into the center comes out clean, about 1 hour. Transfer to a rack to cool.

TANGERINE CREAM CHEESE

3   *cups tangerine juice*

½   *pound cream cheese, at room temperature*

Finely grated zest of 4 tangerines

Put the tangerine juice in a medium saucepan and boil over medium heat until it reduces to about ¼ cup of thick syrup, 25 to 30 minutes. Cool to room temperature. In a food processor with the metal blade, or with a whisk, whip the cream cheese until smooth and light. Continue whipping while slowly adding the tangerine syrup, then stir in the zest. Refrigerate until ready to use.

Cut the pound cake into ½-inch-thick slices, and toast them under the broiler until golden on both sides. Spread with cream cheese, and cut each slice into fingers or small triangles.

COCONUT SHORTBREADS

This variation on the classic shortbread recipe is enriched with shredded coconut. You can bake the cookies up to several days in advance, storing them in an airtight container at room temperature.

The quantities below yield about 20 cookies, and the recipe easily doubles, triples, or more.

¾   *pound unsalted butter, softened*

½   *cup brown sugar*

¼   *cup granulated sugar*

2   *eggs*

2   *cups cake flour*

1   *cup shredded coconut*

In a mixing bowl, cream together the butter and sugars. Beat in the eggs one at a time, then combine the flour and coconut and stir it into the creamed mixture just long enough to form a soft dough. Cover the bowl with plastic wrap and refrigerate for 1 hour.

Preheat the oven to 350 degrees F. On a floured surface, roll out the dough to a thickness of ¼ inch. With a cookie cutter, cut the dough into 3-inch rounds. Transfer the rounds to an ungreased baking sheet, and bake until golden brown, 10 to 12 minutes. Cool on a wire rack.

SESAME CHICKEN SKEWERS WITH ORANGE-GINGER GLAZE

Asian in inspiration, these quickly prepared, sesame-encrusted little kebabs of chicken breast are a perfect complement to green or oolong teas.

You'll find the black sesame seeds—a common Japanese ingredient—and the bamboo or wooden skewers in gourmet supply shops, Asian markets, or in the Asian foods section of well-stocked supermarkets.

SESAME CHICKEN SKEWERS

2   *boneless, skinless chicken breast halves (about 7 ounces each)*

½   *cup sesame seeds*

¼   *cup black sesame seeds*

3   *tablespoons olive oil*

1   *tablespoon sesame oil*

1   *teaspoon salt*

1   *teaspoon finely chopped fresh cilantro*

¼   *teaspoon cayenne pepper*

Cut the chicken breasts lengthwise into 12 equal strips. In a mixing bowl, toss the strips with the sesame seeds and seasonings. Thread each strip on a 6- to 8-inch-long wooden or bamboo skewer, patting it with any remaining sesame seeds to make sure it is well crusted. Set the skewers aside.

ORANGE-GINGER GLAZE

½   *cup orange marmalade*

¼   *cup water*

2   *tablespoons finely grated fresh ginger*

1   *tablespoon finely chopped fresh cilantro*

1   *tablespoon sushi (rice wine) vinegar*

Combine all glaze ingredients in a small saucepan over medium heat and simmer for 5 minutes. Puree in a food processor or blender and strain. Set aside.

Before serving, preheat the grill or broiler until very hot. Cook the skewers about 4 inches from the heat source, for 1½ minutes per side or until golden brown.

Lightly brush each skewer with some of the glaze. Serve immediately, with extra glaze on the side for dipping.

Pecan Caramel Tartlets. Coconut Shortbreads. Banana-Fig Toast with Tangerine Cream Cheese.

SMOKED-SALMON-AND-CUCUMBER SANDWICHES ON ONION BREAD

Smoked salmon sandwiches are a staple of the tea table. Here, they are enhanced by a freshly baked onion bread. If you don't have time for the baking, substitute a good-quality onion bread or other bread from a local bakery.

ONION BREAD

1　 *packet active dried yeast*

½　 *cup warm water*

4　 *cups bread flour*

⅔　 *cup finely chopped onion*

¼　 *cup finely chopped fresh chives*

2　 *teaspoons salt*

1　 *egg*

¼　 *cup milk*

2　 *tablespoons vegetable oil*

Stir the yeast into the water, and leave at room temperature about 10 minutes to activate.

Combine the flour, onion, chives, and salt in an electric mixer with the dough hook (or by hand, see page 30). With the mixer running on its slowest speed, pour the yeast and remaining ingredients into the flour mixture, and knead the dough until smooth and elastic, about 10 minutes.

Cover the bowl securely with plastic wrap, and leave it at warm room temperature until doubled in bulk, about 1½ hours. Punch the dough down, empty onto a floured work surface, and shape it into an oblong loaf. Place in a greased 2-quart loaf pan, cover loosely with a kitchen towel, and let rise at room temperature until doubled in bulk, about 1 hour.

Place a baking pan on the oven floor, and pre-heat the oven to 400 degrees F. Put the risen loaf in the oven and, being extremely careful to avoid the steam, immediately pour ½ cup of water into the baking pan at the bottom of the oven.

Bake the bread until it is well risen and golden and sounds hollow when rapped with a knuckle, about 40 minutes. Do not open the oven door during the first 20 minutes of baking. Cool to room temperature on a wire rack before slicing.

SMOKED SALMON-CUCUMBER FILLING

¾　 *cup mascarpone*

½　 *pound thinly sliced smoked salmon*

2　 *medium-size seedless cucumbers, thinly sliced crosswise*

To make the sandwiches, cut 6 lengthwise slices of bread, ¼ inch thick, from the loaf. Thinly spread one side of each slice with mascarpone. Place the salmon in a single layer on 3 of the slices. Thinly spread the mascarpone over the salmon. Place the cucumbers, overlapping slightly, on top. Cover with the remaining bread slices. With a sharp knife, cut the sandwiches into a variety of small shapes and arrange on a serving platter.

DRY SHERRY

Offer guests a small glass of dry sherry—preferably a *fino* variety. In case they prefer something slightly sweeter, have a bottle of Amontillado on hand as well.

This fountain graces the center courtyard at the Hotel Bel-Air.

Coupes and Coffee on the Terrace

Serves 6 to 8

I<small>N A GRAND</small> E<small>UROPEAN TRADITION THAT PREDATES THE CUSTOM OF TEATIME, THE</small> B<small>EL</small>-A<small>IR OFFERS A</small> late-afternoon assortment of glorious ice cream coupes to relax over on the terrace with a cup of coffee. A choice of two of the hotel's most popular sundaes is presented here, both created with freshly made ice cream and sauces. If you like, feel free to substitute the best-quality store-bought ice cream you can find.

B<small>ANANA</small>-B<small>LACK</small> W<small>ALNUT</small> C<small>OUPE</small>

C<small>OUPE</small> M<small>ADEIRA</small>

S<small>ELECTION OF</small> H<small>OT</small> C<small>OFFEES</small>

BANANA-BLACK WALNUT COUPE

A rich banana ice cream with black walnuts and an intense praline sauce contribute an old-fashioned quality to this particular sundae.

The quantities given here are enough for 8 sundaes.

BANANA ICE CREAM

1	cup heavy cream
½	cup milk
8	egg yolks
⅔	cup sugar
2	very ripe large bananas, pureed
1	cup coarsely chopped and roasted black walnuts

In a saucepan, bring the milk and cream to a boil over medium heat. Meanwhile, gradually whisk together the egg yolks and sugar until smooth and light lemon colored. Stir briskly into the boiling milk mixture, then set the bottom of the pan in an ice water bath, stirring frequently until the mixture cools. Stir in the banana.

Process in a commercial ice cream maker, following the manufacturer's directions. When the ice cream is almost done and still somewhat soft, stir in the walnuts. Transfer to the freezer and freeze for at least 4 hours.

PRALINE SAUCE

¾	cup brown sugar
½	cup granulated sugar
¼	cup heavy cream
3½	tablespoons unsalted butter
1	tablespoon bourbon

Put the sugars, cream, and butter in a heavy saucepan and bring to a boil, stirring, over moderate heat. Remove from the heat and, when the sauce has cooled to lukewarm, stir in the bourbon.

TOPPINGS

½	cup whipping cream
2	teaspoons sugar
1	teaspoon bourbon
2	ripe bananas, cut into ¼-inch slices
½	cup roasted and chopped black walnuts

Whip the cream with the sugar until soft peaks form. Whisk in the bourbon.

To assemble the sundaes, scoop 4 ounces of the ice cream into each sundae glass. Pour 3 tablespoons of the warm sauce over each serving. Top with sliced bananas, whipped cream, and a sprinkling of black walnuts.

COUPE MADEIRA

The exotic flavors of rum-soaked raisins and a caramel sauce spiked with Madeira make this a very beguiling ice cream creation.

The quantities given here are enough for 8 sundaes.

1	quart Rum Raisin Ice Cream (recipe on page 63)
1½	cups Caramel Madeira Sauce (recipe on page 63)
1½	cups whipped cream
½	cup toasted pine nuts
½	cup bittersweet chocolate shavings

Scoop 4 ounces of the ice cream into each sundae glass. Pour 3 tablespoons of the sauce over each serving. Top with whipped cream, and sprinkle with pine nuts and chocolate shavings.

SELECTION OF HOT COFFEES

Strong, hot coffee is the quintessential European accompaniment to an ice cream coupe. Select a robust, fairly dark, afternoon-style blend such as Viennese, brewed by the drip or plunger-pot methods. Offer cream and sugar, though black coffee offers a perfect foil to the rich sweetness of the ice cream.

If you are fortunate enough to own an espresso maker, brew strong espresso to serve with the coupes, offering guests the option of cappuccino or *caffe latte*.

Each room at the Hotel Bel-Air has its own private entrance.

CHINESE TEA BASKET

Serves 1 or 2

WHEN GUESTS CHECK INTO THE BEL-AIR, A CHINESE-STYLE TEA BASKET AWAITS THEM AS A greeting in their room—its bright silk lining hugging a porcelain tea pot and two glasses, one filled with sliced lemon, the other with sugar cubes. In winter, the pot is filled with hot passion fruit tea; in the summer, the same tea is iced. The basket itself sits on a wicker tray with china tea cups and a small assortment of the hotel's teatime treats, including freshly baked scones. A bowl of fresh fruit and a glass jar of dried fruits completes the welcome.

While it isn't necessary to duplicate such a presentation item by item at home, any small show of attentiveness such as this goes a long way. Shortly before your overnight guests arrive, set out a tray with tea pot, cups, and a few things to nibble on—whether scones, their favorite chocolates, or some of the other tea items on pages 82 to 88. With little effort, you'll have made them feel especially welcome.

PASSION FRUIT TEA

CURRANT SCONES

FRESH AND DRIED FRUITS

PASSION FRUIT TEA

Oolong tea flavored and scented with dried passion fruit has fast become a favorite beverage in Southern California and is widely available at gourmet markets and shops.

For hot tea, brew it following the directions on page 84. For iced tea, brew it in advance, adding about 1 teaspoon extra per pot to make the tea somewhat stronger; strain the tea, cool to room temperature, then chill in the refrigerator. Return the cold tea to a chilled tea pot with a generous handful of ice cubes.

Though the tea, hot or cold, is naturally sweet, offer guests sugar and lemon to add to their cups if they wish.

The gardens of the Hotel Bel-Air provide the perfect surroundings for relaxing with a cup of tea.

CURRANT SCONES

Though these classic scones are outstanding straight out of the oven, you can bake them up to a day ahead and reheat them for 5 minutes in a 200 degree F oven before serving with strawberry jam and butter or whipped cream.

The quantities here yield 8 scones, and the recipe easily doubles or triples.

2	cups all-purpose flour
¾	teaspoon baking soda
½	tablespoon cream of tartar
	Pinch of salt
8	tablespoons chilled unsalted butter, cut into small pieces
½	cup currants
1	egg, lightly beaten
½	cup buttermilk
1	egg yolk
1	tablespoon milk

Preheat the oven to 425 degrees F. In a mixing bowl, stir together the flour, baking soda, cream of tartar, and salt. Cut in the butter until the mixture resembles coarse crumbs. Stir in the currants. Add the egg and buttermilk and stir very lightly, just until the ingredients are combined.

On a well-floured surface, roll out the dough to a ½-inch thickness. Cut out rounds with a 2½-inch cutter and place on a lightly greased and floured baking sheet. Beat together the egg yolk and milk, and brush it over the tops of the scones. Bake until well risen and golden, 12 to 15 minutes. Serve warm.

FRESH AND DRIED FRUITS

Alongside the tea tray, present a bowl of fresh seasonal fruits—just a few specimens each of whatever is in peak condition at your market. Include a good table knife and a plate for guests to slice the fruit if they wish.

In a glass jar that shows off their shapes and colors, also present an assortment of good-quality dried fruits: peach, apricot, and pear halves; whole figs and prunes; and wedges of pineapple and spears of papaya.

CHAPTER FIVE

DINNER

ROMANTIC TERRACE SUPPER AT TWILIGHT
Serves 2

A S NIGHT DESCENDS ON THE GROUNDS OF THE HOTEL BEL-AIR, THE TERRACE BECOMES THE perfect spot for a romantic meal—especially at one of the intimate alcove tables overlooking Swan Lake. No wonder, then, that this is a favorite setting for Valentine dinners, marriage proposals, and anniversary celebrations.

To complement the mood, this three-course menu is composed of luxurious, seductive dishes: fresh seafood, pheasant in a vibrant red cherry sauce, and ultra rich crème brulée. With some careful advance preparation, it is a fairly easy meal to make at home for a loved one. Set the table with your finest china, silver, and crystal, turn the lights low, and light some candles. And if the weather is pleasant, by all means move the table outdoors to the terrace, patio, or garden.

ROAST PHEASANT WITH SWEET POTATO CROQUETTES, WARM FIELD GREENS,
AND SUN-DRIED CHERRY SAUCE

CALIFORNIA BOUILLABAISSE

MANGO-COCONUT CRÈME BRULÉE

Wine suggestion:

With the bouillabaisse, serve a rich Chardonnay, such as Flora Springs "Barrel-Fermented," Kistler, Woltner, or Long. You could continue drinking the Chardonnay with the pheasant, though a Pinot Noir would go very well with the cherry sauce. Try one from Sanford, Byron, or Morgan, in California; or, for a change of pace, sample an Oregon Pinot such as Ponzi Reserve, Rex Hill, or Elk Cove.

ROAST PHEASANT WITH SWEET POTATO CROQUETTES, WARM FIELD GREENS, AND SUN-DRIED CHERRY SAUCE

Main course, vegetable, and salad all appear together on a single plate in this elegant presentation of dynamic colors and shapes: a crescent of pale white pheasant breast, a mound of multicolored greens, two amber orange cylinders of sweet potato, and the deep red of a fruit sauce imbued with the intense flavor of sun-dried cherries. (Produced in Michigan, sun-dried cherries are now distributed in gourmet shops nationwide.)

Elaborate though the dish looks, its preparation is very straightforward. The croquettes, made from a fairly fragile mixture, require preparation up to a day in advance so that they can be piped and frozen; an hour or two before serving time, they are cut into individual pieces, breaded and prefried, to be recrisped just before serving. (The quantities below yield about 10 croquettes, but they freeze well.)

You can stuff the pheasant and prepare the aromatic vegetable base on which it roasts several hours ahead of time, so the pheasant will be ready to start cooking 45 minutes to 1 hour before serving. The sauce, which takes just 20 minutes or so to prepare, may be started while the pheasant roasts. The simply dressed salad is tossed just before it goes on the plate.

SWEET POTATO CROQUETTE MIXTURE

1½	cups cold baked and mashed sweet potatoes (2 to 3 medium)
¼	cup instant mashed potato powder
2	eggs
¼	cup heavy cream
3	tablespoons maple syrup
1	teaspoon chopped fresh thyme
1	teaspoon chopped fresh chives
½	teaspoon salt
¼	teaspoon white pepper

Put the sweet potato and potato powder in a food processor, and pulse briefly to blend. Add the remaining ingredients, and pulse until thoroughly blended. Transfer to a medium saucepan, and stir over moderate heat just until the mixture thickens to a soft, pastelike consistency, 5 to 7 minutes. Remove from the heat, and cool to room temperature.

To shape the croquettes, pack the mixture into a pastry bag fitted with a ¾-inch straight tip. On a lightly oiled baking sheet, pipe the mixture into long, straight lines. Cover very loosely with waxed paper and freeze several hours, until hard.

An hour or two before serving time, heat 2 to 3 inches of vegetable oil in a deep, heavy pan or deep fryer to 350 degrees F on a deep-frying thermometer.

CROQUETTE COATING

2	eggs
2	tablespoons water
2	cups all-purpose flour
2	cups dried bread crumbs

Assemble the breading ingredients, beating together the eggs and water. With a sharp knife, cut the frozen lines of sweet potato into 3-inch pieces. Bread them immediately, rolling each piece in flour to coat it well, then dipping in egg and rolling in bread crumbs. As soon as the croquettes are coated, carefully drop them into the hot oil and fry until golden brown, 3 to 5 minutes. With a wire skimmer, transfer them to paper towels to drain; leave at room temperature until ready to serve.

ROAST PHEASANT

2½- to 3-pound pheasant, drawn	
1	sprig fresh thyme
1	sprig fresh rosemary
3	whole garlic cloves, crushed
	Salt to taste
	Freshly ground black pepper to taste
1	tablespoon unsalted butter
1	medium onion, coarsely chopped
1	celery stalk, coarsely chopped
1	carrot, coarsely chopped

Stuff the bird with the thyme, rosemary, and garlic, and season thoroughly inside and out with salt and pepper. Preheat the oven to 350 degrees F.

In a medium skillet, melt the butter over moderate to high heat. Add the onion, celery, and carrot, and sauté until golden brown, 5 to 7 minutes. Transfer the vegetables to a roasting pan, reduce the heat to moderate, and put the pheasant in the pan. Turn the pheasant in the pan until lightly browned all over, 4 to 5 minutes. Place the bird breast-up in the roasting pan. Roast until the juices run clear when the thickest part of the thigh is pierced with a thin skewer, about 25 minutes.

Remove the bird from the oven and let it rest in the pan for about 15 minutes.

SUN-DRIED CHERRY SAUCE

5	whole black peppercorns
1	sprig fresh thyme
1	whole clove
1	1-inch piece cinnamon stick
½	medium garlic clove
½	medium shallot
⅓	cup cranberry juice
⅓	cup apple juice
⅓	cup water
⅓	cup sun-dried cherries

While the pheasant is cooking, prepare the sauce. Securely tie the peppercorns, thyme, clove, cinnamon, garlic, and shallot in a piece of cheesecloth. Put the bag in a medium saucepan with the juices and water, bring to a boil, reduce the heat, and simmer 5 minutes.

Add the cherries to the pan and simmer gently for 10 minutes more. Then remove the pan from the heat, and let the sauce steep for 5 minutes.

Remove the cheesecloth bag, and puree the sauce in a blender or processor. Then pass it through a fine sieve, adding a little warm water if necessary to give it a thin, syrupy consistency.

When the sauce is almost done, reheat the deep-frying oil to 350 degrees F. Carefully drop the croquettes back into the oil, and fry for 30 seconds to heat them through. Drain on paper towels.

WARM FIELD GREENS

1 *tablespoon olive oil*

1 *teaspoon sushi (rice wine) vinegar*

1½ *cups mixed baby field greens (Romaine, curly endive, upland cress, spinach, red oak lettuce, mizuna, tatsoi, or other baby leaves) at room temperature*

¼ *cup fried leeks (recipe on page 78)*

 Salt to taste

 Freshly ground black pepper to taste

Combine the oil and vinegar in a mixing bowl. Toss well with the baby greens and the fried leeks and season.

To serve, cut the two thighs away from the pheasant; strip off and discard their skin, pull the meat off the bone and, with a sharp knife, cut it into ¼-inch-thick julienne strips. Cut the two breast halves whole from the carcass; strip off their skin, and carve each crosswise on a bias into ½-inch-thick pieces.

 Fan a pheasant breast in a crescent across the bottom of each serving plate. Arrange a pile of thigh meat at the center of the plate, and mound the salad high on top of it. Cross 2 croquettes at the top of each plate. And, just before serving, spoon several tablespoons of the sun-dried cherry sauce around the edges of the sliced breast meat.

Roast Pheasant with Sweet Potato Croquettes, Warm Field Greens, and Sun-Dried Cherry Sauce.

CALIFORNIA BOUILLABAISSE

Seafood stars in this variation on the classic Provençal fish soup, garnished with braised fennel and leeks, slices of sourdough baguette spread with grilled eggplant, and an aioli sauce enhanced with fresh basil. Depending on what is available, you can substitute equal quantities of other seafood for those listed.

Though there are a lot of separate parts to the bouillabaise, apart from the final cooking of the fish, each element can be made well in advance, to be combined when you do the final cooking just before you serve it.

SEAFOOD BROTH

¼	cup olive oil
½	cup diced red bell pepper
½	cup finely chopped bulb fennel
¼	cup finely chopped celery
3	tablespoons finely chopped shallots
6	medium garlic cloves, finely chopped
¾	cup dry white wine
2	tablespoons finely chopped Italian parsley
1	tablespoon salt
5	whole black peppercorns
4	sprigs fresh thyme
2	bay leaves
¾	cup chopped tomatoes
¼	cup brandy
3	cups chicken stock
2	cups water
1	cup fish trimmings (bones, heads, and lobster shells only)
1	teaspoon finely grated lemon zest

In a 2-quart saucepan, heat the olive oil over moderate heat. Add the bell pepper, fennel, celery, shallots, and garlic. Sauté, stirring frequently, for 10 minutes.

Add the wine, parsley, salt, peppercorns, thyme, and bay leaves. Simmer for 5 minutes. Add the tomatoes and brandy and cook 5 minutes more. Add the stock, water, and fish trimmings, and simmer for 45 minutes.

Strain the broth through a double layer of cheesecloth, discarding the solids. Stir in the lemon zest and set aside.

SEAFOOD

2	black mussels
2	pieces Pacific halibut fillet
1	baby coho salmon fillet, cut in half on the bias
1	small Pacific or Maine lobster tail split in half lengthwise
2	fresh basil sprigs (for garnish)

Bring 2 cups of the broth to a boil in a medium saucepan; reduce the heat to a simmer, add the lobster, and cook for 30 seconds. Add the halibut, salmon, and mussels and remove from the heat. Cover, and leave for 5 minutes.

With a slotted spoon, transfer the seafood to warmed soup plates; add the leeks and fennel Vegetable Garnish to the plates. Bring the broth back to a simmer and ladle it over the fish. Garnish with croutons and basil sprigs; serve Aioli on the side, to be spooned into the broth.

BASIL AIOLI

1	medium garlic clove
1	egg yolk
½	slice white bread, crust trimmed
2	teaspoons lemon juice
½	teaspoon salt
½	cup olive oil
10	fresh basil leaves

Put the garlic, egg yolk, bread, lemon juice, and salt in a food processor with the metal blade, and process until finely pureed. With the machine running, slowly pour in half the oil. Add the basil leaves and pulse the machine until blended. Then, with the machine running, slowly pour in the remaining oil to build a thick emulsion. Store, covered, in the refrigerator; bring to room temperature before serving.

VEGETABLE GARNISH

1	tablespoon olive oil
1	medium fennel bulb, trimmed and cut into 6 wedges
4	baby leeks, trimmed to about 4 inches, roots trimmed away but root ends left intact
½	teaspoon salt
1½	cups chicken stock

Heat the oil in a small saucepan over high heat. Add the vegetables and sauté for 3 minutes. Season with the salt, add the chicken stock, and reduce the heat to medium. Simmer until the leeks are tender, 8 to 10 minutes, then remove. Continue simmering until all the stock has evaporated and the fennel is tender, 5 to 10 minutes more. Set the vegetables aside.

GRILLED EGGPLANT CROUTONS

1	¼-inch-thick slice of eggplant, peeled
	Olive oil
	Salt to taste
	Freshly ground black pepper to taste
1	teaspoon chopped fresh thyme
2	slices sourdough baguette, ⅓ inch thick, cut on the bias

Preheat the broiler. Brush the eggplant on both sides with olive oil, season to taste with salt and pepper and sprinkle with thyme; broil on both sides until tender and golden, about 5 minutes total. Finely dice the eggplant. Lightly brush the bread with olive oil, and broil on both sides until golden. Spread one side of each slice with the diced eggplant, then cut each slice in half lengthwise.

California Bouillabaisse

MANGO-COCONUT CRÈME BRULÉE

Crème brulée, one of the most seductively rich of desserts, gets added appeal here from the rich flavor of coconut and cubes of rum-marinated mango.

You can prepare the dessert several hours in advance, waiting to add and caramelize the final burnt-sugar coating just before serving.

For ease of preparation, the quantities below yield 3 servings—enough to share an extra if you both crave seconds. The recipe also multiplies easily.

½   ripe mango, peeled and cut into ½-inch cubes

¼   cup dark rum

2½   cups heavy cream

1   cup shredded coconut

     Pinch of ground allspice

4   egg yolks

6   tablespoons brown sugar

     Superfine sugar

     Fresh berries (for garnish)

     Mint sprigs (for garnish)

In a mixing bowl, toss the mango with the rum. Cover, refrigerate, and marinate for 2 hours.

In a medium saucepan, stir together the cream, coconut, and allspice. Bring to a boil over moderate heat. Remove from the heat, and leave to steep for 10 minutes. Then strain out the coconut, pressing hard with a wooden spoon to extract all the liquid from the shreds.

Preheat the oven to 250 degrees F. In another bowl, whisk together the egg yolks and brown sugar until they form ribbons when the whisk is lifted out. Gradually beat the warm coconut cream into the yolks.

Place 3 individual-serving shallow custard cups, about 5 inches in diameter, in a baking pan. Add cold water to the pan to come halfway up the sides of the cups. Distribute the mango among the cups, then pour in the coconut custard mixture. Put the pan in the oven, and bake for 20 minutes.

Carefully remove the pan from the oven, and lift out the custard cups. Let them cool to room temperature, then refrigerate until serving time.

Before serving, preheat the broiler until very hot. Lightly sprinkle superfine sugar onto each custard to cover its entire surface. Place the cups under the broiler as close to the heat as possible, just until the sugar turns an even caramel brown, 30 seconds to 1 minute. Serve immediately.

Wine Suggestion:

With the salmon, offer a dry California Gewürztraminer such as those from Z. Moore or Navarro. The seafood panache needs a brash young Chardonnay; those from Matanzas Creek or Grgich Hills would be excellent.

Squab calls for a big, rustic red with some spiciness to it. Worth exploring is a new blend of Cabernet Sauvignon, Cabernet Franc, and Merlot grapes, generally known as "Meritage." Iron Horse's Cabernets, Cain's "Cain 5," and Mondavi-Rothschild's "Opus I" are fine examples.

The veal would be wonderful with a nice red Burgundy from France—a Gevry Chambertin from Alain Burget, Joseph Roty, or Phillipe LeClerc. A California Cabernet is the perfect choice for the lamb: Try Silver Oak, Spottswood, Beringer Reserve, or Shafer "Hillside Select."

With the dessert, sample one of California's excellent dessert wines: one of the late-harvest Rieslings from Chateau St. Jean or Joseph Phelps, a late-harvest Gewürztraminer from Bonny Doon, or a vintage port from Quady.

A Wine Tasting in the Main Dining Room
Serves 12

With a wine list offering well more than 500 different vintages from the United States, France, Italy, and Germany, it's only natural that the main dining room at the Bel-Air is the frequent scene of gala wine-tasting dinners, at which half a dozen or so different outstanding bottles are paired with small portions of some of the kitchen's most renowned recipes.

A complicated menu such as the one that follows takes meticulous advance preparation if the host plans to spend much time at the table with the guests. If you are at all uncertain about coordinating the work, cut down on the number of courses (and the number of people you invite, since the portion sizes are deliberately small); or, for such a gala occasion, consider hiring some kitchen help for the evening.

Chill the white wines well in the refrigerator or an ice bucket before serving. Serve the red wines at cool room temperature, and open the bottle an hour or so before pouring to encourage the development of their bouquets.

To offer guests the opportunity to taste and compare all the wines, be sure to set as many glasses at each setting as there are wines being served; this may well require renting some glasses. And, while the luxury of the evening may well call for candlelight along with your finest tableware, don't turn the lights down too low: Allow ample illumination for the color and clarity of each wine to be appreciated to the fullest.

Petite Veal Tenderloin Medallion with Truffle Oil and Braised Baby Leeks

Pan-Roasted Peppered Baby Lamb Chop and Minipotato Gallette with Balsamic Vinaigrette

Ginger-Marinated Salmon with Shiitake Mushroom "Chopsticks"

Grilled Squab with Fried Garlic Noodles

Panache of Lobster and Shrimp with Lime-Cilantro Sauce

Mascarpone Sorbet

Petite Veal Tenderloin Medallion with Truffle Oil and Braised Baby Leeks

PETITE VEAL TENDERLOIN MEDALLION WITH TRUFFLE OIL AND BRAISED BABY LEEKS

The delicate flavor of high-quality veal is magnificently complemented by the perfume of truffle oil, which is available at most good gourmet shops and markets.

Allow about 1 hour to cook the sauce, which may be made farther in advance and gently reheated before serving. The phyllo baskets that hold the leeks may also be made an hour or two ahead of time and held at room temperature in an airtight container. Start cooking the leeks while you preheat the grill or broiler to cook the veal.

SWEET RED PEPPER-FENNEL SAUCE

1   tablespoon olive oil

3   tablespoons finely chopped red bell pepper

2   teaspoons finely chopped fennel bulb

2   teaspoons finely chopped shallots

1   teaspoon fennel seed

1   teaspoon Hungarian paprika

¼   cup white wine

4   cups veal or chicken stock

2   tablespoons diced red bell pepper

2   tablespoons diced bulb fennel

      Salt to taste

      Freshly ground black pepper to taste

Heat the olive oil in a medium saucepan over low heat. Add the chopped bell pepper, fennel, and shallots and sauté 1 minute. Add the fennel seed and paprika and sauté 1 minute more. Add the wine and simmer 1 minute. Add the stock and simmer gently until the liquid reduces to 1 cup, about 1 hour.

While the sauce is reducing, blanch the diced pepper and fennel in boiling water for 1 minute. Drain. When the sauce is reduced, strain out the solids, add the blanched vegetables, and season with salt and pepper. Set aside.

PHYLLO BASKETS

3   full sheets packaged phyllo dough

3   tablespoons melted unsalted butter

Preheat the oven to 350 degrees F. Place 1 sheet of the dough on a clean, dry work surface, and brush it lightly with 1 tablespoon of butter. Place a second sheet on top and brush it with butter. Repeat with the third sheet and remaining butter.

Cut the layered dough lengthwise into thirds, then crosswise into quarters, to make 12 layered rectangles. Gently press each rectangle into a 2-ounce muffin cup. Bake until golden, about 10 minutes. Set aside.

BRAISED LEEKS

1   tablespoon olive oil

¾   cup baby leeks, thinly sliced on the bias

¼   cup white wine

1   sprig fresh thyme

½   teaspoon salt

¼   teaspoon white pepper

¾   cup chicken stock

¼   cup asparagus, thinly sliced on the bias

2   tablespoons finely diced carrot

3   tablespoons heavy cream

Heat the oil in a small saucepan over moderate heat. Add the leeks and sauté for 3 minutes. Add the wine, thyme, salt, and pepper, and simmer until the liquid evaporates, 5 to 7 minutes. Add the chicken stock, and simmer until reduced to a thick, syrupy consistency, 10 to 12 minutes. Remove the thyme sprigs. Add the asparagus, carrot, and cream, raise the heat to high, and cook 1 minute more. Keep warm.

VEAL MEDALLIONS WITH TRUFFLE OIL

12   2½-ounce veal tenderloin medallions

Salt to taste

Freshly ground black pepper to taste

2   tablespoons truffle oil

12   fresh parsley sprigs (for garnish)

Preheat the grill or broiler until very hot. Season the veal with salt and pepper, and grill or broil until medium, about 5 minutes per side.

To serve, spoon 1½ tablespoons of Sweet Red Pepper-Fennel Sauce in the center of each plate. Spoon the Braised Leeks into the Phyllo Baskets. Place a veal medallion on top of the sauce, and a phyllo basket to one side. Drizzle truffle oil over the medallions. Garnish with parsley sprigs.

PAN-ROASTED PEPPERED BABY LAMB CHOP AND MINIPOTATO GALLETTE WITH BALSAMIC VINAIGRETTE

Inside each of these quickly sautéed little chops is a small sliver of Parmesan cheese, whose flavor—along with that of the cracked peppercorn coating—subtly enhances the natural taste of the lamb.

The mint sauce and the little sliced potato cakes, or gallettes, that accompany the chops are very easily made in advance and held until serving time.

POTATO GALLETTES

3   medium baking potatoes

¾   cup olive oil

Salt to taste

White pepper to taste

Peel the potatoes and pare each down to a 1½-inch-diameter cylinder. Then cut each cylinder crosswise into very thin round slices.

In a small nonstick skillet, carefully place a circular arrangement of potato slices, each overlapping the previous one by half, to form a ring about 2½ inches across. Season lightly with salt and pepper, and quickly form another ring on top of the first. Season again. Add ¼ cup of the oil. Sauté until the bottom is golden brown, about 4 minutes. Carefully flip the gallette, and sauté until the other side is golden brown, 3 to 4 minutes more. Transfer to paper towels to drain. Pour off excess oil and remove for next gallette. Repeat with the remaining slices until you have completed 12 gallettes.

MINT SAUCE

3   tablespoons finely chopped fresh mint

2   tablespoons sushi (rice wine) vinegar

1   tablespoon lime juice

1   teaspoon finely chopped fresh thyme

1   teaspoon finely chopped fresh shallots

1   teaspoon bottled chili sauce

1   teaspoon salt

1   egg yolk

6   tablespoons olive oil

3   tablespoons hazelnut oil

Put all the ingredients but the oils in a food processor or a blender, and process until smoothly combined. With the machine running, slowly pour in the oils to build a thick emulsion. Set aside.

PEPPERED LAMB CHOPS

12   baby lamb chops

12   small slivers Parmesan cheese

1½   tablespoons finely cracked black peppercorns

1½   tablespoons finely cracked white peppercorns

3   tablespoons olive oil

3   tablespoons diced tomato (for garnish)

12   small mint sprigs (for garnish)

With a small, sharp knife, carefully cut a narrow slit in the side of each lamb chop near the bone; insert a sliver of Parmesan into each chop. Toss together the cracked peppercorns, and dip both sides of each chop in the mixture to coat it lightly.

Heat half of the olive oil in a medium skillet, over high heat, until it begins to smoke. Place 6 chops in the skillet and sear them for 1 minute; then turn and sear 45 seconds to 1 minute more. Remove the chops and set them aside. Add the remaining oil, heat it, and cook the remaining chops.

To serve the chops, spoon 2 tablespoons of the Mint Sauce in the center of each plate. Arrange the tomato around the plate. Place a Potato Gallette near the center of the plate, to one side, and place a lamb chop next to it. Garnish with a mint sprig.

GINGER-MARINATED SALMON WITH SHIITAKE MUSHROOM "CHOPSTICKS"

Sweet soy sauce and fresh ginger enhance the flavor of fresh salmon in this Asian variation on the classic Scandinavian gravlax.

Begin curing the salmon at least 2 full days ahead of time; it will keep well, covered in the refrigerator, for up to 2 weeks. Prepare and prefry the "chopsticks"—actually thinly rolled, deep-fried wonton skins—an hour or so in advance, and then crisp them up just before serving.

GINGER-MARINATED SALMON

1	pound kosher salt
1	cup granulated sugar
¼	cup coarsely grated fresh ginger root
3	tablespoons white pepper
2	fresh serrano chiles
2	bunches fresh cilantro leaves
1	pound center-cut piece fillet of salmon, skin left on
1	cup sweet soy sauce

Put all the ingredients, except the salmon and sweet soy, in a food processor with the metal blade. Process until well combined and finely chopped. In a glass or ceramic dish just large enough to hold the salmon, pack the salmon on all sides, skin-side up, with the curing mixture. Cover with plastic wrap and refrigerate for 24 hours.

Remove the salmon from the curing mixture. Rinse lightly, pat dry, and discard the curing mixture. Clean out the dish, fill it with the sweet soy, and return the salmon to the dish, basting well; keep the salmon skin-side up, so that the surface of its flesh remains in contact with the soy. Cover with plastic wrap and refrigerate 24 to 48 hours, until the salmon is stained a deep brown color.

Remove the salmon from the soy, pat dry, wrap in cheesecloth, and refrigerate until serving.

Before serving, cut 24 paper-thin slices on the bias from the cured fillet.

SHIITAKE MUSHROOM "CHOPSTICKS"

¼	cup peanut oil
3	dozen fresh shiitake mushroom caps, finely chopped
2	finely chopped serrano chiles
2	tablespoons finely chopped fresh cilantro
1	teaspoon finely grated fresh ginger root
3	tablespoons soy sauce
3	tablespoons sake
12	large fresh wonton skins
1	egg, lightly beaten

Heat the peanut oil in a large skillet over moderate heat. Add the mushrooms and sauté for about 5 minutes. Add the chiles, cilantro, and ginger, and sauté 2 to 3 minutes more. Add the soy and sake and cook, stirring occasionally, until all the liquid has evaporated and the mixture is fairly dry, 5 to 7 minutes more. Remove from the heat and cool to room temperature.

Cut the wonton skins diagonally in half to form 24 triangles. Brush each skin lightly with beaten egg. Put the filling in a pastry bag, and pipe a thin line of it along the longest side of each triangle. Tightly roll up the triangles into pencil shapes. Refrigerate.

Heat 2 to 3 inches of vegetable oil in a deep, heavy pan or deep-fryer to 350 degrees F on a deep-frying thermometer. A few at a time, taking care to keep them from becoming misshapen, slip the chopsticks into the oil and fry until very lightly browned, about 2 minutes. Drain on paper towels and set aside.

PRESENTATION

2	tablespoons mustard powder
1	tablespoon sour cream
1	tablespoon water
2	tablespoons sweet soy sauce
2	tablespoons peanut oil
1	tablespoon sesame oil
1	tablespoon sushi (rice wine) vinegar
½	teaspoon finely chopped garlic
¼	teaspoon salt
	Pinch of white pepper
3	cups mixed baby greens (see page 103), at room temperature
3	tablespoons julienned daikon (Japanese white radish)
3	tablespoons julienned red bell pepper
3	tablespoons fresh chives cut into 1½-inch pieces
2	tablespoons julienned yellow bell pepper

In a small bowl, stir together the mustard powder, sour cream, and water. With a fork, randomly drizzle this sauce on the serving plates. With another fork, drizzle the sweet soy sauce on the plates. Place two slices of salmon on one half of each plate.

Stir together the peanut and sesame oils, vinegar, garlic, salt, and white pepper to make a dressing. Toss the baby greens and remaining ingredients with the dressing and place a small mound of salad at the top of each plate.

Reheat the deep-frying oil to 350 degrees F. Carefully drop the chopsticks back into the oil, and fry for 30 seconds to heat them through and brown them. Drain on paper towels, and place two, crisscrossed, on the left side of each plate.

Ginger-Marinated Salmon with Shiitake Mushroom "Chopsticks"

GRILLED SQUAB WITH FRIED GARLIC NOODLES

Asian flavors combine with a contemporary French nouvelle style of presentation in this flavorful course.

The most difficult part of a fairly easy preparation is the boning of the squab. You can ask your butcher to do it for you, making sure that he saves you all the bones and the trimmings to use in the sauce. The sauce itself requires about 1 hour of cooking; you can make it farther in advance and gently rewarm it before serving. And though the noodles take just a matter of minutes to prepare, you can make them as far in advance as you like, since they are equally good served hot or at room temperature.

GRILLED SQUAB

6	whole squabs, drawn
6	tablespoons fragrant peanut oil
2	tablespoons chopped fresh cilantro
1	tablespoon chopped fresh mint
1	tablespoon freshly ground black pepper
2	teaspoons sesame oil
2	teaspoons chopped fresh thyme
2	teaspoons finely grated fresh ginger root
2	tablespoons salt

Cut the birds into breasts with wings attached and legs with thighs attached. Bone the breast and wing portions, trimming off the last joint of the wings and leaving the single wing bones attached to the breasts. Remove the bones from the thighs, leaving in the leg bones. Reserve all trimmings and bones.

In a glass or ceramic dish large enough to hold the breasts and legs, toss together the remaining ingredients for the squab, except the salt. Add the breasts and legs and toss well to coat. Cover and leave at cool room temperature or refrigerate.

SAUCE

3	tablespoons peanut oil
	Bones and trimmings from the squabs
3	tablespoons finely chopped shallots
2	medium garlic cloves, finely chopped
3	cups well-reduced chicken stock (simmered down from 6 cups)
3	tablespoons black vinegar
3	tablespoons sushi (rice wine) vinegar
1	tablespoon soy sauce
2	teaspoons salt
1	teaspoon red chili flakes
1	sprig fresh thyme

Heat the oil in a large saucepan over moderate heat. Add the squab bones and trimmings, and sauté until evenly browned, about 10 minutes. Add the remaining sauce ingredients, and simmer gently until the liquid reduces by half, about 1 hour. Strain out the solids and keep warm; or refrigerate, to reheat gently before serving.

RED PEPPER PUREE

½	cup chicken stock
¼	cup chopped red bell pepper

Bring the stock with the peppers to a boil in a medium saucepan. Reduce the heat and simmer 10 minutes. Puree in a food processor or blender, and strain through a fine sieve. Set aside.

FRIED GARLIC NOODLES

4	whole medium garlic cloves
2	4-ounce packages chuka soba noodles (available at Asian markets or well-stocked supermarkets)
⅓	cup scallions, thinly sliced on the bias
4	tablespoons finely julienned red bell pepper
3	tablespoons fresh chives, cut into 2-inch pieces
1	tablespoon peanut oil
2	teaspoons finely chopped fresh cilantro
1½	teaspoons finely grated orange zest
1	teaspoon sushi (rice wine) vinegar
1	teaspoon soy sauce
2	teaspoons black sesame seeds
	Salt to taste
	Freshly ground black pepper to taste
	Cilantro sprigs (for garnish)

Put the garlic cloves in a small saucepan of cold water. Bring to a boil. When the cloves are cool enough to handle, peel and thinly slice them. Heat about 1 inch of vegetable oil in a heavy skillet. Add the sliced garlic, and fry until light golden brown, about 2 minutes, taking care not to overcook them. Remove with a wire skimmer, and drain on paper towels.

Cook the noodles in boiling water until al dente, following package directions. Drain well. In a mixing bowl, toss the noodles with the garlic and remaining ingredients. Set aside.

Add the salt to the marinating squab and toss well. Preheat the grill or broiler until very hot.

Wipe the excess marinade from the squab. Put the squab pieces on the grill or the broiler tray with the skin side facing the heat. Grill close to the heat for about 4 minutes; then turn and grill 2 to 3 minutes more, until medium-rare.

To serve, mound the noodles in the center of the plates. Place a squab breast and leg on either side of the noodles. Spoon about 2 tablespoons of the warm sauce over the meat. Using a fork, streak the plates randomly with the pureed bell pepper. Garnish the noodles with cilantro.

Grilled Squab with Fried Garlic Noodles

Panache of Lobster and Shrimp with Lime-Cilantro Sauce

PANACHE OF LOBSTER AND SHRIMP WITH LIME-CILANTRO SAUCE

This colorful seafood pasta presentation offers an intense combination of flavors: the richness of the seafood and the sharp tastes of contrasting cream sauces.

Both sauces can be made in advance and stored in the refrigerator. The cilantro sauce will be left cold, the lime sauce gently rewarmed before serving. As soon as you start boiling the pasta, begin the final preparation of the lobster and shrimp.

CILANTRO SAUCE

½	cup chicken stock
½	cup heavy cream
5	tablespoons finely chopped fresh cilantro
1	teaspoon finely chopped shallot
½	teaspoon salt
¼	teaspoon white pepper
1	small garlic clove, finely chopped
3	tablespoons blanched and chopped fresh spinach

Stir together all the ingredients, except the spinach, in a medium saucepan. Bring to a boil over moderate heat and reduce by half. Put the mixture in a blender or food processor with the spinach and puree. Pass through a fine strainer, cover, and chill in the refrigerator.

LIME SAUCE

1½	cups chicken stock
½	cup heavy cream
¼	cup white wine
3	tablespoons finely chopped fresh cilantro
2	tablespoons roasted and pureed red bell pepper
1	tablespoon finely chopped shallots
1	teaspoon salt
¼	teaspoon white pepper
	Juice and finely grated zest of 2 limes
1	teaspoon corn starch
1	tablespoon cold water

Stir together all the ingredients except the corn starch and water in a medium saucepan, and bring to a boil over moderate heat. Simmer briskly until reduced by half. Dissolve the corn starch in the water and stir it into the sauce; cook 1 minute until slightly thickened. Pass through a fine strainer. Keep warm if being served shortly; or cover and refrigerate, to be reheated gently before serving.

PANACHE OF LOBSTER

3	tablespoons olive oil
12	large raw shrimp, peeled and deveined
12	small lobster claws, shelled, or ¼-inch-thick lobster tail medallions, blanched in boiling water for about 1 minute
1	teaspoon finely chopped shallots
¼	cup white wine
	Salt to taste
	Freshly ground black pepper to taste
3	tablespoons red and yellow bell peppers, diced into ⅛-inch pieces
½	small garlic clove, finely chopped
1	cup cooked linguine
1½	tablespoons finely chopped fresh chives
1	teaspoon finely chopped fresh cilantro
½	teaspoon finely chopped fresh mint
	Fresh cilantro sprigs or chives (for garnish)

Place half the oil in a large skillet over moderate heat. Add the shrimp and sauté for 45 seconds; add the lobster, shallots and wine, and cook 15 seconds more. Season with salt and pepper. Cook about 15 seconds more, then check the shrimp to see if they are done; if not, remove the lobster and simmer about 15 seconds more.

In a small saucepan over moderate heat, heat the remaining oil. Add the peppers and garlic and sauté about 10 seconds. Add the cooked linguine, herbs, and salt and pepper to taste; toss well.

For each serving, spoon 2 tablespoons of the warm Lime Sauce in the center of each plate. Drizzle about 1 tablespoon of the Cilantro Sauce on top. Distribute the pasta on top of the sauce. Place 1 shrimp and 1 piece of lobster on either side of the pasta. Garnish with cilantro or chives.

MASCARPONE SORBET

Rich yet light, this dessert resembles ice cream, especially because it is based on tangy and creamy Italian mascarpone cheese. Yet it is made in the style of a sorbet, which results in a sublimely velvety texture.

Scoop the sorbet into iced dishes or glasses and garnish, if you like, with fresh seasonal berries.

The sorbet may be made a day or two in advance. The quantities below yield about 3 quarts.

1	quart water
2¼	cups sugar
1	ounce glucose syrup or light corn syrup
1	pound mascarpone, at room temperature
3	ounces white port
	Juice of 1 lemon

In a medium saucepan, stir together the water, sugar, and glucose over moderate heat. Boil for 5 minutes, then remove from the heat and cool to warm room temperature.

Stir the remaining ingredients into the sugar syrup. Process in an ice cream maker, following manufacturer's instructions.

A Birthday Dinner
Serves 4

A SPECIAL FAMILY OCCASION LIKE A BIRTHDAY CALLS FOR OUT-OF-THE-ORDINARY DISHES THAT excite comment: new, surprising tastes, unusual combinations, and dazzling presentations. These dinner specialties from the Bel-Air menu more than meet those exalted specifications, providing a sensational celebration on The Terrace, in The Restaurant, or in a private suite.

At home, the menu offers the added advantage of being very easy to prepare, with lots of simple planning done well in advance and very quick last-minute cooking. Even the elaborate-looking special dessert—individual tarts of poached pear on a puff-pastry base—is done almost entirely in advance, though you have the option of putting them in the oven to bake just over half an hour before you plan to serve them.

BELGIAN ENDIVE WITH PEARS, BRIE, AND TOASTED ALMOND VINAIGRETTE

GRILLED SWORDFISH WITH LOBSTER NOODLES, CUCUMBERS, AND RED CHILI VINAIGRETTE

WARM ARTICHOKE AND ASPARAGUS SALAD WITH
SMOKED GOAT CHEESE ON CRISP POTATO RINGS

INDIVIDUAL PEAR TARTS WITH PEAR CREME ANGLAISE

Wine suggestion:

Before the meal and with the first course, pour Champagne—Krug or Veuve-Clicquot's Yellow Label—or a fine California sparkling wine, such as Roederer Estate or Schramsberg. With the vegetable salad, serve a dry California Riesling such as Trefethen, or try the excellent Washington State dry Riesling from the Hogue.

The swordfish calls for a high-acid Chardonnay with overtones of tropical fruit, such as those from Sanford, ZD, or Cambria. With the pear tart, pour one of the California late-harvest wines from Chateau St. Jean or Joseph Phelps, or a fine French Sauternes or German Trockenbeerenauslese.

Belgian Endive with Pears, Brie, and Toasted Almond Vinaigrette

Quickly prepared, this elegant little appetizer contrasts the rich, distinctive flavor of Brie cheese with the sweetness of pear and the slight bitter edge of Belgian endive.

Almond Vinaigrette

¼ cup blanched almond

½ cup vegetable oil

2 tablespoons apple cider vinegar

1 teaspoon sherry vinegar

1 teaspoon salt

¼ teaspoon white pepper

Spread the almonds on a baking sheet and toast in a 350 degree F oven until golden, 5 to 7 minutes. Put them warm into a food processor with a metal blade, and process until they form a coarse paste. Add the oil and process 1 minute. Add the remaining ingredients and pulse to blend.

Endive, Pears, and Brie

¾ cup mixed baby greens (see page 103)

2 Belgian endives, cut crosswise into ½-inch-wide pieces

1 Comice pear, peeled, cored, and julienned

2 tablespoons julienned carrot

2 tablespoons julienned raw beet, rinsed well and drained

¼ cup 2-inch-long pieces of fresh chive

½ teaspoon salt

¼ teaspoon white pepper

8 small wedges Brie

1 tablespoon diced tomato

1 teaspoon chopped fresh thyme

8 whole chives (for garnish)

To assemble the servings, distribute all but 2 tablespoons of the dressing on the bottoms of 4 plates. In a mixing bowl, toss together the greens, endive, pear, carrot, beet, and chives. Add the remaining vinaigrette, salt, and pepper, and toss briefly again.

Mound the vegetable mixture in the center of each plate and place 2 Brie wedges at the bottom. Sprinkle lightly with tomato and thyme, and garnish with whole chives.

To assemble the servings, distribute all but 2 tablespoons of the dressing on the bottoms of 4 plates. In a mixing bowl, toss together the greens, endive, pear, carrot, beet, and chives. Add the remaining vinaigrette, salt, and pepper, and toss briefly again.

Mound the vegetable mixture in the center of each plate and place 2 Brie wedges at the bottom. Sprinkle lightly with tomato and thyme, and garnish with whole chives.

Grilled Swordfish with Lobster Noodles, Cucumbers, and Red Chili Vinaigrette

Like much Asian-influenced cuisine, this distinctively seasoned dish of grilled swordfish and stir-fried lobster noodles is cooked very quickly.

Start the swordfish marinating an hour or two before cooking. While the grill heats up, assemble all the remaining ingredients, having them ready to combine and cook at the last minute before serving.

Grilled Swordfish

3 tablespoons fragrant peanut oil

1 tablespoon finely chopped fresh ginger

1 tablespoon finely chopped fresh thyme

½ tablespoon freshly ground black pepper

1½ pounds trimmed swordfish loin fillets, cut into eight 3-ounce pieces

Cucumber and Garnish

1 seedless cucumber, peeled and thinly sliced crosswise

1 tablespoon fresh chives, cut into ½-inch pieces

Stir together the peanut oil, ginger, thyme, and pepper in a glass or ceramic dish large enough to hold the swordfish pieces. Toss the swordfish pieces in the mixture to coat them evenly; cover and refrigerate for 1 to 2 hours.

Before serving, preheat the grill or broiler until very hot. Overlap the cucumber slices to completely cover the bottom of each serving plate and set aside.

Put the swordfish on the grill or broiler close to the heat and cook for 3 minutes per side, until medium.

Lobster Noodles

2 tablespoons fragrant peanut oil

1 8- to 10-ounce lobster tail, blanched, shelled, diced into ½-inch pieces

6 tablespoons red bell pepper roasted and diced into ¼-inch pieces

2 teaspoons finely chopped fresh cilantro

1 small garlic clove, finely chopped

1 4-ounce package chuka soba noodles, cooked al dente following package instructions, drained

Salt to taste

Freshly ground black pepper to taste

While the swordfish is cooking, prepare the lobster noodles. Heat the peanut oil in a medium skillet over moderate heat. Add the lobster, red pepper, cilantro, and garlic to the skillet and sauté 1 minute. Add the drained noodles and salt and pepper to taste. Toss well and remove from the heat.

Red Chili Vinaigrette

5 tablespoons fragrant peanut oil

2 tablespoons sushi (rice wine) vinegar

1 tablespoon sesame oil

1 tablespoon sugar

2 teaspoons red chili flakes

1 teaspoon finely chopped fresh cilantro

1 teaspoon salt

Juice and finely grated zest of 1 lime

Whisk together all the vinaigrette ingredients.

To serve, lightly season the cucumbers on each plate with salt and pepper. Place 2 pieces of swordfish at the center of each plate. Divide the noodles in their skillet into 4 equal portions and, with a fork, spin each portion of noodles into a rough coil, and transfer it to the plate next to the swordfish. Scatter pieces of the lobster mixture from the pan over the mounds of noodles. Drizzle about 2 tablespoons of vinaigrette over the swordfish and cucumbers. Garnish with chives.

Grilled Swordfish with Lobster Noodles, Cucumbers, and Red Chili Vinaigrette

WARM ARTICHOKE AND ASPARAGUS SALAD WITH SMOKED GOAT CHEESE ON CRISP POTATO RINGS

Three luxurious vegetables—artichoke heart, chanterelle mushrooms, and asparagus tips—combine in this quickly sautéed and elegantly composed warm salad, served atop an ultrathin layer of crisp potato.

With the growing popularity of goat cheese, a creamy smoked version is becoming more readily available at markets with good cheese selections. If you can't find it, substitute a fresh, creamy goat cheese or one marinated in olive oil and herbs.

The potato rings for the salad can be made several hours in advance, to be rewarmed briefly in the oven while you cook the vegetables.

CRISP POTATO RINGS

3   *medium baking potatoes*

1   *cup oil*

    Salt to taste

    Freshly ground black pepper to taste

Peel the potatoes and slice them very thinly. In a small, nonstick omelet pan, place the potatoes overlapping in the pan to form a 5-inch-diameter ring. Overlap a few more slices to fill in the center. Season lightly with salt and pepper.

Add ¼ cup of the oil and over moderate heat sauté until golden, 4 to 5 minutes. Carefully turn the potato ring over, and cook 3 to 4 minutes more until crisped on the other side. Drain on paper towels, and repeat with the remaining potatoes and oil. Set the potato rings aside. Before serving, preheat the oven to 250 degrees F. Put the potato rings on a baking sheet and warm them in the oven for 3 minutes.

Warm Artichoke and Asparagus Salad with Smoked Goat Cheese on Crisp Potato Rings

WARM ARTICHOKE AND ASPARAGUS SALAD WITH SMOKED GOAT CHEESE

2	tablespoons olive oil
½	cup chanterelle mushrooms, cut lengthwise into ¼-inch slices
2	prepared artichoke bottoms, cut into 4 wedges
20	2-inch-long asparagus tips
¼	cup chicken stock
2	teaspoons finely chopped shallots
1	teaspoon finely chopped fresh chives
1	teaspoon finely chopped fresh Italian parsley
½	teaspoon finely chopped fresh thyme
½	teaspoon finely chopped fresh tarragon
2	Roma tomatoes, peeled, halved, and seeded
	Salt to taste
	Freshly ground black pepper to taste
⅔	cup mixed baby greens (see page 103)
2	tablespoons Balsamic Vinaigrette (recipe on page 52)
4	oval, 1-ounce scoops smoked creamy goat cheese

Heat the oil in a small skillet over moderate heat. Add the chanterelles and sauté for 30 seconds. Add the artichoke, asparagus, chicken stock, shallots, and herbs. Cook until the stock evaporates, about 30 seconds more. Add the tomato pieces, season with salt and pepper, toss well, and set aside.

While the potatoes are being heated, toss the greens with 1 tablespoon of the vinaigrette, seasoning with salt and pepper.

Place a potato ring on the center of each serving plate. Imagining the ring like a clock, place a tomato half near the ring's edge at 12 o'clock. Place ¼ of the pieces at 3; some chanterelles at 6; some asparagus at 9; and the goat cheese at 11. Mound the greens in the center, and drizzle the remaining vinaigrette over the vegetables and around the potato.

INDIVIDUAL PEAR TARTS WITH PEAR CRÈME ANGLAISE

These beautiful little pastries have just the right touch of elegance for a special celebration.

The crème anglaise may be made several hours ahead and refrigerated in a covered bowl. While the tarts are wonderful eaten warm out of the oven, they are also excellent if baked a few hours in advance and served at room temperature.

PEAR CRÈME ANGLAISE

1	cup half-and-half
1	whole vanilla bean, split in half lengthwise
4	egg yolks
⅓	cup sugar
3	tablespoons pear brandy (Pôire William)

Put the half-and-half in a medium saucepan, and scrape the seeds from the vanilla bean into the pan, adding the bean shells too. Bring to a boil over moderate heat. Remove from the heat and set aside.

In a mixing bowl, beat the egg yolks and sugar together until they are pale yellow in color and form ribbons when the whisk is lifted from the bowl. Stir a few tablespoons of the hot half-and-half into the yolks, then gradually pour and stir the yolk mixture into the pan of half-and-half.

Return the pan to very low heat and cook, stirring continuously, until the mixture is thick enough to coat the back of a wooden spoon, 7 to 10 minutes. Place the bottom of the pan in ice water, and stir to cool the mixture down and arrest cooking. Pour the crème through a fine sieve, transfer to a bowl, stir in the pear brandy, cover, and refrigerate.

FRANGIPANE

¼	pound almond paste
¼	cup unsalted butter, softened
2	tablespoons sugar
2	egg yolks
¼	cup all-purpose flour
1	tablespoon pear brandy (Pôire William)

Knead together the almond paste and butter until smooth. Add the remaining ingredients, and stir or knead to a smooth paste. Set aside.

PEAR TARTS

2	cups water
1	cup sugar
1	cinnamon stick
1	whole clove
2	large Bartlett pears, peeled, halved, and cored
1	pound puff pastry, defrosted
2	egg yolks
2	tablespoons milk

Bring the water, sugar, cinnamon, and clove to a boil in a medium saucepan. Add the pear halves and simmer until tender-crisp, about 10 minutes. Remove the pears from the syrup, drain on kitchen towels, and cool to room temperature.

To assemble the tarts, roll out ¾ pound of the Frangipane pastry on a floured surface to a ¼-inch thickness. With the tip of a small, sharp knife, cut out 4 pear-shaped pieces of pastry about ½ inch larger all around than the pear halves. Roll out the remaining pastry to a ⅛-inch thickness, and cut it into long ⅛-inch-wide strips.

Preheat the oven to 350 degrees F.

Place a pear half cut side down on each of the 4 pastry cutouts. Drape the thin strips of pastry over the pears to form a lattice, pressing them against the rim of the bottom piece of pastry and crimping up its sides. Attach ½- to ¾-inch-long pastry strips to the stem end of the pastry base to imitate pear stems. Beat together the egg yolks and milk, and brush them over the pastry.

Carefully transfer the tarts to a greased baking sheet, and bake until the pastry is golden brown, about 30 minutes. Serve warm or at room temperature, accompanied by the chilled Pear Crème Anglaise.

A Late-Night Supper in the Bar

Serves 4

LATE INTO THE EVENING IN THE COMFORTABLE, FIRELIT BAR AT THE BEL-AIR, GUESTS CAN ORDER from a menu of dishes more casual but no less beautiful or delicious than the fare served just next door in the main dining room.

This simple, late-night menu is easy and fun to prepare at home, served as, say, an après-theater or after-the-movie supper for a few friends. All the preparation is done in advance, earlier in the day. Within 20 minutes or so of returning home, the meal is ready to eat. Serve it on the coffee table, by the fireside, or, if there is room enough, even in the kitchen—so that guests can keep you company while you do the cooking.

SPICY FRENCH FRIES

BURRITO OF GRILLED MARINATED CHICKEN AND GUACAMOLE WITH TOMATILLO SALSA

PASSION FRUIT, GRAPEFRUIT, AND CACTUS PEAR SORBETS WITH BERRY SALSA

Wine suggestion:

Offer a cool, spicy, and somewhat acidic young red: from France, a Chateauneuf du Pape such as Pignon or Vieux Telegraph; from California, a Zinfandel such as those from Louis Martini or Joseph Phelps. Alternatively, this is a great menu for beer: Try a Mexican one, such as Bohemia, or a selection from California's new boutique breweries, such as Eureka, Pacific Coast, or Sierra Nevada.

SPICY FRENCH FRIES

A blend of spices coats these crisp shoestring fries with zesty—but not too hot—flavor.

You can blanch the fries in oil earlier in the day and hold them at room temperature. The spiced salt can also be blended in advance and kept at room temperature in a covered bowl.

SHOESTRING FRIES

3   medium baking potatoes

2   quarts vegetable oil (for deep-frying)

Peel and cut the potatoes lengthwise into ¼-inch shoestrings. As they are cut, put them in a large bowl of cold water.

In a heavy 1-gallon pot or deep-fryer, heat the oil to 250 degrees F on a deep-frying thermometer. Drain the potatoes. To avoid splattering, pat them thoroughly dry with paper towels. In 2 separate batches, fry the potatoes until pale brown, about 5 minutes per batch. Drain on paper towels, reserving the oil.

SPICY SALT

2   tablespoon kosher salt

¾   teaspoon ground cumin

¾   teaspoon freshly ground black pepper

½   teaspoon finely chopped fresh parsley

½   teaspoon ground coriander

½   teaspoon cayenne pepper

Stir together the ingredients and reserve.

Shortly before serving, heat the oil to 350 degrees F on a deep-frying thermometer. In 2 batches, fry the potatoes again until golden brown, 3 to 5 minutes per batch. Drain well on paper towels, toss with the spice mixture, and serve immediately.

The Bar at the Hotel Bel-Air provides a cozy place to dine.

BURRITO OF GRILLED MARINATED CHICKEN AND GUACAMOLE WITH TOMATILLO SALSA

This Mexican favorite probably gets its name—"little burro"—from the plump round shape of the rolled flour tortilla and from the ample cargo it is capable of carrying: in this case, a filling of marinated and grilled chicken breast, roasted sweet corn, and a spicy guacamole.

You can make the guacamole, roast the corn, and start the chicken marinating early in the day. All that is left to do is grill the chicken and assemble the burritos just before serving.

TOMATILLO SALSA

1   tablespoon olive oil

3   medium garlic cloves, finely chopped

2   shallots, halved

8   medium tomatillos, quartered

1 to 3 fresh serrano chiles, seeded,
     and finely chopped

⅓   cup chopped tomatoes

¼   cup chicken stock

     Salt to taste

     Freshly ground black pepper to taste

     Juice of 2 limes

1   tablespoon finely chopped fresh cilantro

Make the salsa up to a day ahead of time. Heat the oil in a small saucepan over moderate heat; add the garlic and shallots and sauté until lightly browned, about 2 minutes. Add the tomatillos and chiles (1 to 3, depending on how hot you want the salsa) and sauté 2 minutes more. Add the tomatoes and chicken stock and cook 3 minutes more. Transfer to a blender or food processor and pulse until coarsely pureed. Season with salt and pepper, and stir in the lime juice and cilantro. Cover and refrigerate.

MARINATED CHICKEN

     Juice and finely grated zest of 2 limes

3   medium garlic cloves, finely chopped

2   tablespoons sesame oil

1   tablespoon tomato paste

2   teaspoons salt

1   teaspoon finely chopped fresh thyme

1   teaspoon white pepper

1   teaspoon unsweetened cocoa powder

½   teaspoon chili powder

1   pound 2 ounces skinned and boned chicken
     breasts, pounded to a thickness of ½ inch

Start marinating the chicken at least 1½ hours in advance.

In a glass or ceramic dish large enough to hold the chicken, stir together all the marinade ingredients. Add the chicken and turn to coat it completely. Cover and refrigerate.

Shortly before serving, preheat the grill or broiler until very hot. Cook the chicken close to the heat until nicely charred but still juicy inside, 2 to 3 minutes per side. With a large, sharp knife, cut the chicken crosswise into ¼- to ½-inch-wide strips. Toss the strips to separate them.

GUACAMOLE

1   large, ripe Haas avocado, halved, pitted,
     peeled, and coarsely chopped

1   fresh serrano chile, stemmed, seeded, and
     finely chopped

     Juice of 1½ limes

¼   cup finely chopped red onion

3   tablespoons finely chopped tomato

4   teaspoons finely chopped fresh cilantro

1   teaspoon salt

½   teaspoon freshly ground black pepper

Put all the ingredients in a food processor or blender and puree until smooth. Transfer to a bowl and cover with plastic wrap, pressing the plastic down against the surface of the guacamole to help prevent discoloration. Refrigerate.

BURRITO ASSEMBLY

4   8-inch-diameter flour tortillas

4   medium leaves butter lettuce

½   cup kernels cut from roasted sweet corn
     (recipe on page 73)

½   cup diced tomato

Place the tortillas very briefly on the grill or under the broiler, just long enough to heat them without crisping, no more than about 10 seconds per side.

Place the tortillas on the work surface, and spread them lightly with Guacamole to within ½ inch of their edges. Flatten the lettuce leaves and place on the tortillas. Pile the cooked chicken strips in the center. Sprinkle with corn and tomatoes, and top with a generous dollop of Guacamole. Fold in both sides of the tortilla over the filling, then tightly roll up the tortilla away from you to complete the burrito.

Cut each burrito in half on the bias, and serve with Tomatillo Salsa.

PASSION FRUIT, GRAPEFRUIT, AND CACTUS PEAR SORBETS WITH BERRY SALSA

The bright colors of these sorbets contrast beautifully with the deep, dark color of the fresh berry salsa.

Make the sorbet a day ahead. The salsa may be prepared several hours in advance. If you'd like an additional festive touch—and if you have some flour tortillas left over from the burritos on this menu—try making the optional honey-drizzled tortilla garnish. The quantities below yield about 1 quart of sorbet.

PASSION FRUIT SORBET

1   *cup water*

1   *cup sugar*

¼   *cup white wine*

¾   *cup pulp scooped from halved ripe passion fruits (about 8 fruits total)*

½   *cup orange juice*

2   *tablespoons aged tequila*

Stir together the water, sugar, and wine in a small saucepan and bring to a boil over moderate heat. Remove from the heat and cool to room temperature.

In a food processor, puree the passion fruit pulp with the orange juice. Press through a strainer to remove the crushed black seeds; reserve 1 tablespoon of seeds.

Stir together the syrup, fruit puree, reserved seeds, and tequila. Process in an ice cream or sorbet maker, following manufacturer's instruction. Transfer to the freezer in a covered container.

GRAPEFRUIT SORBET

1   *cup water*

1   *cup sugar*

¼   *cup white wine*

1¼   *cups fresh grapefruit juice*

2   *tablespoons white tequila*

Stir together the water, sugar, and wine in a small saucepan and bring to a boil over moderate heat. Remove from the heat and cool to room temperature.

Stir together the syrup, grapefruit juice, and tequila. Process in an ice cream or sorbet maker, following manufacturer's instructions. Transfer to the freezer in a covered container.

CACTUS PEAR SORBET

1   *cup water*

1   *cup sugar*

¼   *cup white wine*

1   *pound ripe cactus pears, peeled (wear heavy gloves to avoid any spines)*

2   *tablespoons fresh lime juice*

Stir together the water, sugar, and wine in a small saucepan and bring to a boil over moderate heat. Remove from the heat and cool to room temperature.

In a food processor, puree the cactus pear. Press through a strainer and measure out 1¼ cups of the resulting juice.

Stir together the syrup, cactus pear juice, and lime juice. Process in an ice cream or sorbet maker, following manufacturer's instructions. Transfer to the freezer in a covered container.

BERRY SALSA

⅔   *cup fresh blackberries and raspberries, finely chopped*

4   *tablespoons sugar*

1   *tablespoon aged tequila*

2   *teaspoons finely chopped fresh cilantro*

1   *teaspoon lime juice*

½   *teaspoon finely chopped fresh mint*

1   *small, fresh jalapeño chile, seeded and finely chopped*

Stir together all the ingredients and refrigerate in a covered container.

FRIED TORTILLA TULIPS

Vegetable oil (for deep frying)

2½   *tablespoons honey, at room temperature*

4   *4-inch flour tortillas*

2   *tablespoons confectioner's sugar*

1   *teaspoon ground cinnamon*

Fresh cilantro or mint sprigs (for garnish)

Before serving, heat 3 to 4 inches of vegetable oil in a heavy pan or deep-fryer to 350 degrees F on a deep-frying thermometer. In a small saucepan, gently warm the honey over very low heat just until it is fairly liquid. Using a small stainless steel ladle to hold them under the oil to form a tulip shape, fry the tortillas one at a time until crisp and golden, 30 seconds to 1 minute. Drain on paper towels. Lightly brush the tortillas with the honey. Stir together the sugar and cinnamon and sprinkle over the tortillas.

Place a tortilla tulip on each serving plate. Place 1 small scoop (1½ to 2 ounces each) of each sorbet in each tulip. Spoon 4 tablespoons of salsa around the tortilla on each plate. Garnish with cilantro or mint sprigs.

Passion Fruit, Grapefruit, and Cactus Pear Sorbets with Berry Salsa

Chapter Six

Special Occasions

A Family Thanksgiving
Serves 8

Wine suggestion:

*Offer guests a choice of both
white and red wines with the
meal. For the white, select an
outstanding, big, buttery,
and well-balanced
Chardonnay such as Chalone,
Saintsbury "Reserve,"
Woltner, or Kendall-Jackson
"Proprietor's Reserve." A
light but elegant Pinot Noir—
such as Mondavi "Reserve,"
Calera "Jensen," or Acacia
"St. Clair"—is perfect as the
red wine.*

SINCE THE HOTEL'S EARLIEST DAYS, IT HAS BEEN A TRADITION AMONG LOCAL RESIDENTS TO EAT Thanksgiving dinner at the Bel-Air, where the luxuriance of the gardens and the opulent comfort of The Restaurant provide the perfect atmosphere for celebrating the bounty of life in Southern California. Naturally enough, traditional foods are the bill of fare on the third Thursday in November; but each, of course, has the extra spark of quality and imagination for which the Bel-Air's cooking has always been renowned.

Thanksgiving wouldn't be Thanksgiving without several good hours of work in the kitchen. But this menu is, nevertheless, designed to let the home cook perform a lot of the preparation in advance. And, as in most homes across the nation, it is meant to be served buffet style, with family and friends helping themselves from the overflowing platters. All recipes are easily doubled.

OYSTER STEW WITH SMITHFIELD HAM CROUTONS

CORN-AND-RED-ONION SALAD

ROAST HEN TURKEY WITH SAVORY CORN BREAD-AND-MUSHROOM STUFFING

SMOKED APPLE GIBLET GRAVY

BAKED WINTER SQUASH WITH GARLIC-HERB CRUST

OLD-FASHIONED PUMPKIN PIE WITH CORNMEAL CRUST

PECAN PRALINE ICE CREAM

Oyster Stew

OYSTER STEW WITH SMITHFIELD HAM CROUTONS

An oyster stew seems ideal to start the Thanksgiving feast.

You can make the entire soup base up to a day ahead of time, storing it in the refrigerator. Reheat it just before serving time, adding the vegetable garnish and poaching the oysters the instant before the stew goes to the table. The croutons can be crisped several hours in advance and kept in an airtight container at room temperature.

SOUP BASE

2	tablespoons peanut oil
½	cup coarsely chopped white onion
½	cup coarsely chopped celery
½	cup coarsely chopped carrot
½	cup coarsely chopped green bell pepper
2	tablespoons chopped Smithfield ham scraps
2	tablespoons chopped roasted peanuts
10	whole black peppercorns
4	sprigs fresh parsley
3	sprigs fresh thyme
1	bay leaf
1	small garlic clove, finely chopped
1½	quarts chicken stock
1	cup peeled and diced potato
1	quart milk
½	cup finely chopped fresh spinach leaves

Heat the peanut oil in a 1-gallon pot over moderate heat. Add the onion, celery, carrot, bell pepper, ham, peanuts, peppercorns, parsley, thyme, bay leaf, and garlic. Sauté for 10 minutes. Add the chicken stock and potatoes, and simmer for 30 minutes, until the potatoes are very tender.

With a wire whisk, briskly whisk the soup to puree the potatoes into the liquid. Pour through a very-fine mesh strainer to remove the solids. In a bowl, gradually pour and stir half of the liquid into 2 cups of the milk, then pour this mixture back into the strained liquid. Add the spinach leaves and puree in a processor or blender—in batches, if necessary. Strain again, stir in the remaining milk, and store, covered, in the refrigerator.

SMITHFIELD HAM CROUTONS

16	¼-inch-thick slices French baguette, cut on the bias
¼	cup peanut oil
⅔	cup Smithfield ham, cooked and coarsely pureed
1	tablespoon finely chopped fresh Italian parsley

Preheat the broiler. Brush the baguette slices on both sides with oil. Toast under the broiler until golden brown on both sides. Cool to room temperature, and store at room temperature in an airtight container. In a bowl, stir together the ham and parsley; cover and refrigerate.

VEGETABLE GARNISH AND OYSTERS

½	cup potato, diced into ⅛-inch pieces and blanched in boiling water until al dente, 1 to 2 minutes
⅓	cup carrots, diced into ⅛-inch pieces and blanched in boiling water until al dente, 1 to 2 minutes
¼	cup red bell pepper, diced into ⅛-inch pieces
1½	cups shucked raw oysters
½	teaspoon Tabasco
	Salt to taste
	Freshly ground black pepper to taste

Shortly before serving, return the Soup Base to the pot and bring it to a simmer over low to moderate heat. Meanwhile, spread one side of each crouton with the ham mixture.

Add the Vegetable Garnish to the pot and simmer 1 minute. Add the oysters and cook for 2 minutes more, then season with Tabasco, salt, and pepper. Ladle into heated soup plates, garnish with croutons, and serve immediately.

CORN-AND-RED-ONION SALAD

This simple, fresh-tasting salad makes a bright seasonal addition to the Thanksgiving table.

The corn-and-onion mixture may be prepared, dressed, and refrigerated several hours ahead of time, to be arrayed on its bed of greens just before serving.

CORN-AND-ONION MIXTURE

6	ears sweet corn, roasted in the husk (recipe on page 73), kernels cut from cobs
1½	medium red onions, halved and thinly sliced
1	cup cooked kidney beans
1	cup roasted and diced red bell pepper
2	teaspoons salt
1	teaspoon white pepper
3	tablespoons lime juice
1	tablespoon finely grated orange zest
½	teaspoon ground cumin
1	medium garlic clove, finely chopped
¼	cup olive oil

In a mixing bowl, toss together the corn, onions, kidney beans, and bell pepper. Season with salt and pepper. Add the lime juice, orange zest, cumin, and garlic and toss well. Add the olive oil and toss again. Cover and refrigerate.

MIXED BABY GREENS

3	tablespoons olive oil
2	teaspoons apple cider vinegar
1	teaspoon finely chopped fresh shallots
½	teaspoon salt
3	cups mixed baby greens (see page 103)

Before serving, stir together the oil, vinegar, shallots, and salt. Toss well with the greens. Mound the greens in the center of a serving platter, and surround with the Corn-and-Onion Mixture.

ROAST HEN TURKEY WITH SAVORY CORN BREAD-AND-MUSHROOM STUFFING

A traditional-style corn bread mixture gets the contemporary elaboration of rich, meaty-tasting shiitake mushrooms in the stuffing for this roast turkey.

Bake the corn bread the day before you make the stuffing. For a 15-pound bird, start your final preparations for roasting about 5 hours before dinnertime.

CORN BREAD

2¼	cups all-purpose flour
2¼	cups cornmeal
¼	cup sugar
2	tablespoons baking powder
1	tablespoon salt
3¾	cups milk
½	cup melted unsalted butter
1½	eggs

Prepare the corn bread the day before. Preheat the oven to 350 degrees F. In a mixing bowl, stir together the dry ingredients. In a separate bowl, stir together the milk, butter, and eggs. Stir the liquid ingredients into the dry mixture until thoroughly blended. Pour into a greased and lightly floured 13-by-9-inch baking pan, and bake until golden brown, about 30 minutes. Cool to room temperature, then store overnight in an airtight container.

STUFFING MIXTURE

6	tablespoons olive oil
2	cups pearl onions, blanched in boiling water for 2 to 3 minutes
3	cups thinly sliced button mushrooms
1½	cups thinly sliced fresh shiitake mushroom caps
1½	cups thinly sliced fresh chanterelle mushrooms
1	cup chicken stock
4	medium garlic cloves, finely chopped
2	tablespoons finely chopped fresh chives
1	tablespoon finely chopped fresh basil
1	tablespoon finely chopped fresh tarragon
1	tablespoon finely chopped fresh sage
	Salt to taste
	Pepper to taste

Cut the corn bread into 1-inch cubes, and measure 6 cups of them.

Heat the olive oil in a large skillet over high heat. Add the pearl onions, and sauté until lightly browned, about 2 minutes. Add all the mushrooms, and sauté about 15 seconds. Add the stock and simmer until all the liquid has evaporated, 7 to 10 minutes. Stir in the garlic, herbs, salt, and pepper and cook 1 minute more. Add the 6 cups of corn bread and toss well. Remove from the heat and set aside.

ROAST HEN TURKEY

1	medium celery stalk, coarsely chopped
1	medium carrot, coarsely chopped
1	medium onion, coarsely chopped
1	15-pound fresh hen turkey, drawn, giblets reserved
	Salt to taste
	Freshly ground black pepper
	Paprika to taste

Preheat the oven to 325 degrees F. Spread the celery, carrot, and onion in a large roasting pan. Season the turkey generously inside and out with salt, pepper, and paprika. Stuff the turkey at both ends with the stuffing. (Place any remaining stuffing in a baking dish, to be moistened with a little turkey stock—from the gravy recipe that follows—and bake, covered, for the last 45 minutes of the turkey's roasting time.) Truss the bird and place it in the roasting pan.

Roast the turkey, basting it frequently so that it browns evenly, until the juices run clear when the thickest part of the turkey's thigh is pierced with a thin skewer, about 4 hours. Remove the turkey from the oven, transfer to a carving board or serving platter, and let it rest at room temperature for about 20 minutes before carving. Serve with the stuffing and Smoked Apple Giblet Gravy.

SMOKED APPLE GIBLET GRAVY

Smoked apples contribute remarkable richness and sweetness to this gravy. If you don't wish to rig a home smoker, use plain apples instead.

When you buy your turkey, ask the butcher for turkey trimmings—wings, necks, and backs—for the stock, along with the giblets. Make the turkey stock the day before, letting it cool to room temperature and then refrigerating it. You can also smoke the apples and cook the giblets a day ahead, refrigerating both in a covered dish. The actual making of the gravy, however, has to be done in conjunction with the cooking of the turkey, since roasting pan juices are added to the sauce; read over both recipes carefully before you start, to ensure efficient preparation.

TURKEY STOCK

3	pounds turkey trimmings (wings, necks, and backs)
2	medium celery stalks, cut into several chunks
2	medium carrots, cut into several chunks
1	medium onion, cut into several chunks
1½	gallons water
8	whole black peppercorns
2	bay leaves
2	sprigs fresh thyme

Make the stock a day ahead. Preheat the oven to 350 degrees F. Spread the turkey parts in a roasting pan, and roast until lightly browned, about 30 minutes. Add the vegetables and continue roasting until the turkey parts are well browned, 15 to 20 minutes more.

Transfer the turkey and vegetables to a 2-gallon stockpot. Place the roasting pan on top of the stove over moderate heat, add 2 to 3 cups of the water, and stir and scrape to deglaze the pan. Pour the deglazing liquid into the stockpot. Add the remaining water, peppercorns, bay leaves, and thyme. Bring to a boil over moderate heat, continuously skimming off the foam that rises to the surface, then reduce the heat and simmer gently for 3½ hours. Strain out the solids and reserve the stock.

SMOKED APPLES

4   green apples, quartered and cored

While the stock is simmering, smoke the apples. To rig the smoker, light and burn charcoal briquets outdoors in a small barbecue or a large, heavy, beat-up old pot at least 8 inches deep. Soak smoking chips in water until saturated, then drain well. When the coals are nearly exhausted, scatter the soaked chips on top: They should smoulder, giving up smoke without igniting. If they catch fire, spray with a little water from a spray bottle to douse them. When the smoke is heavy, set a fine-mesh rack at least 8 inches above the chips. Place the apple quarters on the rack and cover loosely with a pot lid that will allow some smoke and heat to escape. Smoke for 15 minutes, then remove the apples and set them aside.

COOKED GIBLETS

6   ounces turkey hearts and gizzards

1   bay leaf

1   tablespoon finely chopped shallots

3   ounces turkey livers

Bring 3 cups of the Turkey Stock to a boil in a medium saucepan; reduce to a simmer.

Add the hearts, gizzards, bay leaf, and shallots and simmer for 20 minutes. Remove the hearts and gizzards with a slotted spoon. Add the livers to the pan, and poach for 3 minutes only, then remove. Return the liquid used for cooking them to the remaining stock. Put all the giblets in a bowl, cover, and refrigerate. When chilled, dice them into ⅛-inch pieces, keeping the liver separate; return to refrigerator.

GRAVY

⅓   cup all-purpose flour

3   fresh green apples, peeled, cored, and diced into ¼-inch pieces

1   tablespoon finely chopped fresh Italian parsley

1   tablespoon finely chopped fresh chives

1   teaspoon finely chopped fresh thyme

     Juice of 1 lemon

Begin the final gravy preparation about 2½ hours before serving time. Bring the turkey stock to a boil. Add the Smoked Apples, reduce the heat, and simmer for 30 minutes. Meanwhile, using a large spoon or bulb baster, carefully remove ⅓ cup of fat from the pan in which the turkey is roasting, and stir it together with the all-purpose flour to make a smooth roux. Slowly stir the roux into the simmering stock until well blended. Continue simmering over very low heat for 1½ hours, regularly skimming any foam or impurities from the surface.

When the turkey is done roasting and the gravy has reduced to about 2 quarts, strain it well. After you've removed the turkey from its roasting pan and discarded its vegetable roasting base, use about 1 cup of the water to deglaze the roasting pan. Return all the gravy and the deglazing liquid to the pot, add the diced hearts and gizzards, and cook about 10 minutes. Add the fresh green apples, herbs, and lemon juice and simmer 2 minutes more. Add the livers and cook 1 minute more. Serve immediately.

BAKED WINTER SQUASH WITH GARLIC-HERB CRUST

Thanksgiving wouldn't be Thanksgiving without some form of baked squash dish. This version is made extra savory from an aromatic breadcrumb topping.

Though the preparation is very simple, you can layer the casserole and toss together its topping several hours in advance. In that case, however, don't heat and pour in the liquids until just before you put the casserole into the oven to bake, making sure to add the topping halfway through the baking.

Start baking the casserole 1 hour before serving time.

GARLIC-HERB CRUST

1½   cups fresh breadcrumbs

¼   cup grated Parmesan cheese

2   tablespoons finely chopped fresh parsley

1   tablespoon caraway seeds, lightly crushed

1   tablespoon sesame seeds

2   teaspoons finely chopped fresh thyme

2   teaspoons finely chopped fresh chives

1   teaspoon finely chopped fresh rosemary

1   teaspoon finely chopped fresh mint

3   medium garlic cloves, finely chopped

     Finely grated zest of 2 lemons

Toss together all the ingredients and reserve.

WINTER SQUASH CASSEROLE

2   medium acorn squash, peeled, halved, seeded, and cut crosswise into ⅛-inch-thick slices

2   medium butternut squash, peeled, halved, seeded, and cut crosswise into ⅛-inch-thick slices

2   medium baking potatoes, peeled, halved, and cut crosswise into ⅛-inch-thick slices

2   medium tomatoes, cored and cut into ⅛-inch-thick slices

1½   tablespoons salt

½   tablespoon white pepper

1   cup chicken stock

1   cup heavy cream

2   small garlic cloves, finely chopped

1   teaspoon finely grated fresh horseradish

1   teaspoon finely chopped fresh thyme

Preheat the oven to 325 degrees F. Grease a 2- to 2½-quart casserole. Starting and ending with acorn squash, arrange the squashes, potatoes, and tomatoes in alternating layers in the casserole, lightly seasoning each layer with the salt and pepper.

In a medium saucepan, gently simmer the chicken stock, cream, garlic, horseradish, and thyme for 5 minutes. Pour over the squash.

Bake the casserole, covered, for 30 minutes. Then spread the crust evenly over the surface of the casserole. Bake, uncovered, for 30 minutes more.

OLD-FASHIONED PUMPKIN PIE WITH CORNMEAL CRUST

The Bel-Air goes one up on tradition by adding a little cornmeal to the pumpkin pie's crust, enriching its flavor and texture.

You can prepare the pie early on Thanksgiving day, to be served cold or at room temperature.

CORNMEAL CRUST

1	cup plus 2 tablespoons all-purpose flour
¼	cup cornmeal
½	teaspoon salt
9	tablespoons unsalted butter, softened
¼	cup ice water

Preheat the oven to 400 degrees F. Lightly stir together all the ingredients in a mixing bowl, just until combined. Gather the dough into a ball and place between 2 sheets of waxed paper. Roll out the dough into an even, 10-inch circle. Peel off the top piece of paper and, with the other, drape the circle into a 9-inch pie plate. Remove the other sheet of paper and gently press the dough into the plate. Trim the edges and, with your fingertips or a fork, form a decorative fluted rim.

Line the crust with aluminum foil, and fill with dried beans or pie weights. Bake for 10 minutes. Remove the foil and beans, and bake until the bottom of the crust is light golden, about 5 minutes more. Remove from the oven and set aside.

PUMPKIN FILLING

1½	cups canned pumpkin puree
1	cup milk
⅔	cup sugar
2	tablespoons maple syrup
½	teaspoon pure vanilla extract
¼	teaspoon grated cinnamon
¼	teaspoon nutmeg
¼	teaspoon salt
4	eggs, separated
8	tablespoons unsalted butter

Stir together the pumpkin, milk, sugar, syrup, vanilla, and spices. Then stir in the egg yolks—reserving the egg whites—until well blended.

In a small saucepan, melt the butter over low heat and continue cooking until it turns nut brown, 5 to 7 minutes. Stir into the pumpkin mixture.

Beat the egg whites until they form firm peaks. Gently fold the pumpkin mixture into the egg whites.

Empty the filling into the prebaked piecrust. Bake at 400 degrees F for 20 minutes. Reduce the heat to 350 degrees F, and bake until the filling is fully set, about 20 minutes more.

PECAN PRALINE ICE CREAM

A rich mixture of caramel and pecans embellishes vanilla ice cream flavored with maple syrup in this perfect companion to pumpkin pie.

Make the ice cream the day before serving. The ingredients below yield about 3 quarts.

PECAN PRALINE MIXTURE

¾	cup sugar
½	cup water
	Pinch of cream of tartar
¼	cup heavy cream
2	tablespoons unsalted butter
1½	cups broken pecan pieces

Put the sugar, water, and cream of tartar in a deep, heavy, narrow-diameter pan. Stir over low heat until the sugar dissolves completely, then place a candy thermometer in the pan, raise the heat, and boil until the syrup turns light caramel in color, about 330 degrees F on the thermometer. While the syrup is boiling, put the cream in another pan and warm over low heat.

As soon as the caramel is ready (330 degrees F), remove it from the heat and dip the bottom of the pan in cold water. Very carefully pour in the cream: It will foam up dramatically. As soon as the foam subsides, stir in the butter with a whisk to blend. Cool to room temperature and stir in the pecans. Set aside.

MAPLE ICE CREAM

1	quart milk
2	cups heavy cream
½	cup maple syrup
3	vanilla beans, split lengthwise, seeds scraped out, seeds and pods reserved
8	egg yolks
¼	cup sugar
¼	cup brandy

In a saucepan, combine the milk, cream, half of the maple syrup, and the vanilla seeds and pods, and bring to a boil over moderate heat. Meanwhile, gradually whisk together the egg yolks, sugar, remaining syrup, and brandy until they form ribbons when the whisk is lifted out.

Strain out the vanilla pods from the milk mixture. Gradually stir about ½ cup of the hot liquid into the yolk mixture, then briskly stir the yolks into the milk mixture.

Set the bottom of the pan in an ice water bath, stirring frequently, until the mixture cools. Process in a commercial ice cream maker, following the manufacturer's directions. When the ice cream is almost done and still somewhat soft, stir in the praline mixture. Transfer to the freezer, and freeze for at least 4 hours before serving.

Old-Fashioned Pumpkin Pie with Cornmeal Crust.

Wine suggestion:

Here's an occasion to serve the very best bottles of wine. Before dinner, pour an outstanding champagne such as Krug, Veuve Clicquot's Yellow Label, or California's Roederer Estate. With the salmon, switch to a great white Burgundy such as Puligny-Montrachet or Chassagne-Montrachet, or an outstanding, rich California Chardonnay, such as Chalone or Mayacamas.

With the prime rib, offer California's new "Meritage" blend of Cabernet Sauvignon, Cabernet Franc, and Merlot grapes, which is featured in Iron Horse's Cabernets, Cain's "Cain 5," and Mondavi-Rothschild's "Opus I." Or pour a great Cabernet Sauvignon from Ridge, Mount Eden, or Mayacamas, or a Merlot from Pine Ridge, Conn Creek, or Cuvaison.

CHRISTMAS DINNER

Serves 10

THE FIRELIT BEL-AIR DINING ROOM TAKES ON A FESTIVE AIR DURING THE HOLIDAYS, PROVIDING the perfect backdrop for a menu featuring traditional foods bright with the colors and flavors of the season. With California's—and the nation's—new awareness of light eating in mind, though, this menu also includes a seafood course that may serve as an alternative or a companion to the heartier course of roast beef.

As for Thanksgiving, this menu requires some diligent work to reproduce at home. Much of the work, however, can be done in advance. With careful planning and study of the recipes, the final cooking and serving will go efficiently. And besides, what better time of year is there for lavishing love and food on family and friends?

SALAD OF JICAMA, POMEGRANATE, AND PECANS WITH ORANGE VINAIGRETTE

PRIME RIB OF BEEF WITH CABERNET PAN SAUCE, ROAST POTATOES, AND SEASONAL VEGETABLE COMPOTE

PAN-SEARED SALMON WITH CREAMED LEEKS AND HERBED APPLE-MUSHROOM COMPOTE

POPPYSEED CAKE WITH EGGNOG CUSTARD, BRANDIED SUMMER FRUITS, AND TANGERINE ICE CREAM

SALAD OF JICAMA, POMEGRANATE, AND PECANS WITH ORANGE VINAIGRETTE

The bright colors and vivid flavors of a classic holiday dish are present in this contemporary, California-style mélange.

Preparation is very simple and fast. The only advance step required is icing the bell pepper strips several hours ahead of time, to ensure exceptional crispness.

SALAD INGREDIENTS

1	cup julienne strips of red, yellow, and green bell peppers
2	cups julienne strips of jicama
1½	cups arugula leaves
1	cup toasted pecan halves
⅔	cup pomegranate seeds
1	teaspoon finely chopped fresh thyme
1	teaspoon finely chopped fresh cilantro
1	teaspoon finely chopped fresh Italian parsley
½	teaspoon cayenne pepper
3	tablespoons walnut oil
	Salt to taste
	White pepper to taste

Three hours before serving, put the peppers in a mixing bowl full of ice and water. Set aside.

Before serving, drain the iced peppers and pat them dry with a kitchen towel. Toss together the peppers with the other vegetables, the pecans, the pomegranate seeds, herbs, and cayenne pepper. Toss with the walnut oil and season to taste with salt and white pepper. Toss again with ⅓ of the dressing. Spread the remaining dressing on the bottom of a serving platter and mound the salad in the center. Serve immediately.

ORANGE VINAIGRETTE

3	cups orange juice
3	tablespoons apple cider vinegar
12	whole black peppercorns
2	medium garlic cloves, peeled
2	sprigs fresh thyme
2	bay leaves
2	whole cloves
1	medium shallot, peeled
2	tablespoons sugar
¾	cup olive oil

An hour or more ahead of time combine the orange juice, vinegar, peppercorns, garlic, thyme, bay leaves, cloves, and shallot in a saucepan and simmer over medium heat until reduced to ⅓ cup of liquid. Strain the juice into a mixing bowl, stir in the sugar, and set over ice. Whisking continuously, slowly pour the olive oil into the juice, forming a thick emulsion. If necessary, whisk in a little water to thin the dressing to pouring consistency.

PRIME RIB OF BEEF WITH CABERNET PAN SAUCE, ROAST POTATOES, AND SEASONAL VEGETABLE COMPOTE

A roast beef with all the traditional trimmings makes a fitting centerpiece for the holiday table. Here, the roast is—somewhat unconventionally—bone-free for easier carving.

While the recipe that follows may look somewhat complicated, each of the various elements in the presentation of the beef and its accompaniments is easily prepared. The detailed instructions ensure that everything will be ready to serve together at precisely the same moment; read them over carefully before proceeding.

ROAST PRIME RIB

3	tablespoons kosher salt
1	tablespoon freshly ground black pepper
2	medium garlic cloves, finely chopped
9	pounds boneless prime rib of beef
3	carrots, coarsely chopped
3	celery stalks, coarsely chopped
2	parsnips, coarsely chopped
1	onion, coarsely chopped
4	sprigs fresh thyme
3	bay leaves

Preheat the oven to 350 degrees F. Combine the salt, pepper, and garlic and rub the mixture all over the meat. Spread the vegetables, thyme, and bay leaves in the bottom of a roasting pan, and put the meat on top. Put the meat in the oven, and baste every 15 minutes or so with the pan drippings.

When the meat has been in the oven about 2 hours, test the temperature at its center with a roasting thermometer: It should measure 110 degrees F (which, after resting, will yield perfectly rare roast beef). Remove the meat from the oven to a serving platter, and let it rest for 30 minutes before carving.

ROAST POTATOES

30	small new potatoes, halved
¼	cup finely chopped fresh parsley
3	tablespoons finely grated fresh horseradish
2	tablespoons finely chopped fresh tarragon
1	tablespoon freshly ground black pepper
1	tablespoon kosher salt
2	teaspoons finely chopped fresh thyme

Begin the potatoes when the meat has been in the oven for 1½ hours. With a large spoon or bulb baster, collect ½ cup of the roast's pan drippings. Toss the potatoes with the drippings and the rest of the ingredients, and place them in another roasting pan in the oven to cook until tender, about 30 minutes. Remove from oven and set aside.

SEASONAL VEGETABLE COMPOTE

5   medium beets, in their skins

20   baby carrots, peeled

3   medium parsnips, peeled and cut into 1-inch
     pieces

2   tablespoons olive oil

1   cup peeled pearl onions

1   cup chicken stock

3   tablespoons balsamic vinegar

20   small brussels sprouts

     Salt to taste

     Freshly ground black pepper to taste

Begin the vegetable compote at the same time that
the potatoes start roasting, putting the beets in with
the potatoes to roast in their skins for 30 minutes.
While they roast, cook the carrots and parsnips in a
vegetable steamer until crisp-tender, about 10 minutes. Set aside. Heat the olive oil in a medium saucepan over moderate heat. Add the onions and sauté 2
minutes, then add the stock and vinegar, reduce the
heat to low, cover lightly, and simmer until the liquid
evaporates to a glaze on the onions, about 30 minutes. While they cook, blanch the sprouts for 2 minutes in boiling water, drain, and set aside. Season to
taste with salt and pepper.

CABERNET PAN SAUCE

1   small onion, finely chopped

1   small carrot, finely chopped

1   celery stalk, finely chopped

5   whole black peppercorns

1   bay leaf

1   sprig fresh thyme

1   medium garlic clove, finely chopped

2   cups Cabernet Sauvignon

2   cups veal stock

     Salt to taste

While the meat rests, begin the sauce. Discard the
cooked vegetables from its roasting pan, and pour off
all but a tablespoon or so of the pan drippings. Add
the raw onion, carrot, and celery, place the pan over
moderate to high heat, and sauté until they are lightly
browned, 3 to 5 minutes. Add the peppercorns, bay

leaf, thyme, and garlic, and sauté 2 minutes more.
Add the wine to the pan, and stir and scrape with a
wooden spoon to dissolve the pan deposits. Add the
veal stock, bring to a light boil, then reduce the heat
and simmer gently until the sauce is reduced by half,
25 to 30 minutes. Season with salt, strain, and transfer to a sauceboat.

While the sauce is reducing and the meat is still
resting, complete the preparation of the garnishes.
Return the Roast Potatoes to the 350 degree F oven

to reheat for 10 minutes. Peel the cooled roast beets
and cut them in half; return them to the oven in
their pan to rewarm. In the saucepan in which the
onions cooked, combine all the vegetables except the
beets, season to taste with salt and pepper, and warm
them over low to moderate heat.

Present the Roast Prime Rib on a large platter, sur-
rounded by the Roast Potatoes and Vegetable Compote and accompanied by the Cabernet Pan Sauce.

PAN-SEARED SALMON WITH CREAMED LEEKS AND HERBED APPLE-MUSHROOM COMPOTE

The garnishes in this elegant presentation showcase the naturally sweet, rich flavor of fresh salmon.

Preparation is remarkably quick and simple. Make the leek compote a few hours in advance, to reheat just before serving. Both the salmon and the compote are cooked just moments before they go to the table.

CREAMED LEEKS

2	tablespoons olive oil
2	cups coarsely chopped leeks (white and light-green parts only)
1	teaspoon salt
½	teaspoon white pepper
¾	cup chicken stock
¾	cup heavy cream

Heat the oil in a medium saucepan over moderate heat. Add the leeks and sauté 1 minute. Season with salt and pepper. Add the chicken stock and cream, and simmer until the liquid has reduced by half, about 10 minutes. Set aside.

APPLE-MUSHROOM COMPOTE

¼	cup olive oil
1	cup fresh chanterelle mushrooms, cut into ¼-inch-thick slices
1	cup fresh shiitake mushroom caps, cut into ¼-inch-thick slices
2	tablespoons finely chopped fresh Italian parsley
1	teaspoon finely chopped fresh thyme
1	small garlic clove, finely chopped
3	tablespoons chicken stock
2	tablespoons white wine
1	medium red apple, peeled, halved, cored, and cut into ¼-inch-thick slices
1	medium green apple, peeled, halved, cored, and cut into ¼-inch-thick slices
1	teaspoon salt
½	teaspoon white pepper
¼	teaspoon red chili flakes
2	tablespoons unsalted butter

Prepare the compote and the salmon at the same time, while also gently reheating the leeks if you have made them in advance.

For the compote, heat the oil in a large skillet over high heat. Add the mushrooms, herbs, and garlic; sauté 10 seconds. Add the stock and wine and cook 20 seconds more. Add the apples, salt, pepper, and chili flakes; sauté 20 seconds. Add the butter; sauté 20 seconds more.

PAN-SEARED SALMON

¼	cup finely chopped fresh tarragon
3	tablespoons finely grated lemon zest
1	tablespoon freshly grated black pepper
10	3- to 4-ounce portions salmon fillet, skinned
1½	tablespoons kosher salt
½	cup vegetable oil
	Fresh tarragon sprigs (for garnish)

Stir together the tarragon, lemon zest, and pepper. Sprinkle evenly over the salmon pieces, then sprinkle with the salt. Heat the oil in a large skillet over high heat. Place the salmon pieces in the skillet, skin-sides down, and sauté until golden brown, about 1½ minutes. Turn them over and sauté 1 minute more.

To serve, spread the Creamed Leeks on a platter. Arrange the salmon pieces on top of the leeks. Garnish with the fresh compote and fresh tarragon sprigs.

Pan-Seared Salmon with Creamed Leeks and Herbed Apple-Mushroom Compote

Poppyseed Cake with Eggnog Custard, Brandied Summer Fruits, and Tangerine Ice Cream

Favorite holiday ingredients and flavors combine to delightful effect in this colorful dessert. While a number of different elements contribute to the overall effect, each on its own is easily prepared in advance, leaving just the final assembly of individual portions before serving.

One key element of the presentation is the brandied summer fruits, which requires that you put them up several months before the holiday season. If you haven't had the chance to do that, substitute the best store-bought brandied fruits you can find.

Brandied Summer Fruits

1½   cups sugar

1½   cups water

3   cups brandy

2   quarts mixed fresh summer fruit (plums, apricots, nectarines, peaches, raspberries, figs), washed, larger fruits halved or quartered, pits discarded

1   vanilla bean, split lengthwise, seeds scraped out and discarded, pod reserved

4   whole cloves

2   2-inch pieces cinnamon stick

Make the summer fruit several months in advance, when they are at their peak. Bring the sugar and water to a boil in a heavy saucepan; reduce the heat and simmer for 2 minutes, then remove from the heat and cool the syrup to 150 degrees F on a candy thermometer. Stir in the brandy. Pack the fruit into a sterilized canning jar. Pour the brandy syrup over the fruit, add the vanilla pod and spices, seal, and refrigerate until ready to use.

Tangerine Ice Cream

2   cups milk

1   cup sweetened condensed milk

1   cup tangerine juice

     Finely grated zest of 1 tangerine

Make the ice cream a day ahead.

Stir together all the ingredients, and process in an ice cream maker, following manufacturer's instructions. Transfer to the freezer.

Eggnog Custard

1   quart milk

2   cups sugar

10   egg yolks

3   whole eggs

¼   cup cake flour

½   cup cornstarch

2   teaspoons nutmeg

2   tablespoons cognac

1   tablespoon rum

Make the custard several hours in advance.

First, bring the milk and half the sugar to a boil in a heavy saucepan over moderate heat. Meanwhile, in a mixing bowl whisk together the egg yolks and whole eggs with the remaining sugar until the mixture forms ribbons when the whisk is lifted out. Slowly whisk about half the hot milk into the eggs, then gradually whip the egg mixture into the remaining milk until thoroughly blended.

In a separate bowl, stir together the cake flour, cornstarch, and nutmeg. Whisk them into the custard mixture until smooth, then whisk in the cognac and rum.

Gently cook the mixture in a hot water bath, stirring continuously, until thick and smooth, about 10 minutes. Cool to room temperature, cover with plastic wrap, and refrigerate until ready to serve.

Poppyseed Cake

2½   cups confectioner's sugar

½   cup unsalted butter, softened

1   tablespoon dark rum

½   teaspoon salt

     Finely grated zest of ½ lemon

6   eggs, separated

1½   cups poppyseeds, coarsely ground in a food processor

¼   cup all-purpose flour

¼   cup finely chopped seedless raisins

Make the cake up to several hours before serving.

Preheat the oven to 375 degrees F. In a mixing bowl, cream together half the confectioner's sugar with the butter, rum, salt, and lemon zest. One at a time, beat in the egg yolks.

In a separate bowl, whisk together the egg whites with the remaining confectioner's sugar until they form soft peaks. Fold the beaten whites into the creamed mixture.

In another bowl, stir together the poppyseeds, flour, and raisins. Fold this mixture into the already-blended ingredients. Pour the batter into a 9-inch round, nonstick cake pan. Bake until a cake tester inserted into its center comes out clean, about 25 minutes. Let it cool briefly in its pan, then unmold onto a lightly sugared surface or a wire rack to cool. Then, with a bread knife, cut the cake horizontally into 3 equal layers, and cut each layer into 10 wedges.

Raspberry Sauce

½   cup raspberries

2   tablespoons plum wine

Puree the raspberries and plum wine together, then strain out the raspberry seeds. Cover and set aside.

To serve, use a fork to drizzle random streaks of Raspberry Sauce on each individual plate. Place 2 wedges of Poppyseed Cake on each plate. Place a generous scoop of Tangerine Ice Cream at the top of the plate and top it with Brandied Summer Fruits. Finally, pipe or spoon the Eggnog Custard in a decorative pattern on each plate.

Poppyseed Cake with Eggnog Custard, Brandied Summer Fruits, and Tangerine Ice Cream

Oscar Night

Serves 6

IN THE LOS ANGELES AREA, EARLY SPRINGTIME BRINGS WITH IT ONE OF THE MOST EAGERLY ANTICI-pated evenings of the year: the Academy Awards. At Hotel Bel-Air, room service booms as those guests who are not actually at the ceremonies order in a selection of foods to enjoy while they watch the spectacle on TV. So as not to distract from a single film clip, envelope opening, or acceptance speech, the foods typically ordered are those that allow for casual eating—such as the classic Bel-Air dishes in this menu.

The recipes that follow are designed to be served buffet-style from your dining table or coffee table. All of the cooking goes quickly enough to be completed after you get home from work and before the first award is given out.

Tortilla Soup

Griddled Crab Cakes with Sweet Corn Puree

Grilled Quail Salad with Wild Mushrooms and Pancetta Lardons

Assorted Ice Creams

Wine suggestion:

Depending on how you wish to treat the evening, there are 3 different options. If you wish to capture the elegance and sparkle of Hollywood, there is champagne or sparkling wine; try one of the widely available California sparklers produced by French vintners, such as Domaine Chandon or Piper Sonoma. Or you could pour a brisk, young California Chardonnay, such as those from Trefethen, Mondavi, or Clos Pegase. The third choice, appropriate for any such casual gathering around the television, is your favorite ice-cold beer.

TORTILLA SOUP

This robust soup is such a longstanding staple of the Bel-Air dining room that, for many years, regulars of the restaurant would eat a bowl of this as their daily lunch.

Though it cooks in about an hour, you can make the soup the night before if you like, reheating it just before serving. Present the broth in a tureen with the garnishes on the side for guests to serve themselves.

CRISP TORTILLAS

Vegetable oil (for deep frying)
8   6-inch fresh yellow or blue corn tortillas, julienned crosswise into ¼-inch-wide strips

In a large, deep, heavy skillet or deep-fryer, heat about 3 inches of oil to 350 degrees F on a deep-frying thermometer. In several batches, cook the tortilla strips in the oil, taking care not to overcrowd them. Fry until crisp and golden, about 1 minute, removing them with a wire skimmer and draining on paper towels. Reserve half of the tortillas in an airtight container.

SOUP

½   cup olive oil
1½   tablespoons ground cumin
1   tablespoon paprika
½   teaspoon cayenne pepper
1   teaspoon ground coriander
1   bay leaf
6   medium garlic cloves, finely chopped
2   cups finely chopped onion
2   tablespoons salt
3   tablespoons finely chopped fresh cilantro
6   cups chicken stock
4   cups chopped tomatoes
½   pound boneless, skinless chicken breast, grilled or poached and cut crosswise on the bias into ¼-inch-wide strips
1   large ripe Haas avocado, quartered lengthwise, peeled, and cut crosswise into ¼-inch-thick pieces
1   cup mixed, shredded, aged Monterey Jack and cheddar cheeses

Heat the olive oil in a large saucepan over moderate heat. Add half of the Tortilla Chips, the spices, and the herbs (except the cilantro); sauté for 2 minutes. Add the garlic and sauté 1 minute more. Add the onion and sauté 3 minutes. Add the salt and 2 tablespoons of cilantro and sauté 2 minutes more. Add the stock and tomatoes and simmer for 1 hour. Then remove the bay leaf and puree the soup in several batches in a blender or food processor, taking care not to overload the work bowl. Strain through a fine sieve.

To serve the soup, heat it over moderate to low heat. Toss together the chicken and the remaining tablespoon of cilantro and add them with the avocado to the soup; simmer 30 seconds. Ladle the soup into bowls and garnish with cheese and the reserved tortilla strips.

GRIDDLED CRAB CAKES WITH SWEET CORN PUREE

Light and moist, these crab cakes have the advantage of being mixed and shaped up to a day ahead of time, to be fried just before serving time. Their sauce and most of their garnishes may also be prepared in advance.

CRAB CAKES

2   cups masa harina (Mexican-style cornmeal)
1   tablespoon olive oil
5   tablespoons diced red bell pepper
1   pound flaked crabmeat
⅓   cup mayonnaise
1   teaspoon finely chopped fresh cilantro
1   teaspoon finely chopped fresh thyme
½   teaspoon salt
¼   teaspoon white pepper
Juice of 1 lime
Finely grated zest of 1 lemon

Spread the masa on a baking sheet, and toast it in a 350 degree F oven until golden brown, about 15 minutes. Remove from the oven and cool.

Heat the olive oil in a small skillet over moderate heat, and sauté the pepper until crisp-tender, about 3 minutes. Cool to room temperature.

In a mixing bowl, combine the peppers with the crabmeat, mayonnaise, and all the seasonings, stirring until well blended. With moistened hands, shape the mixture into 18 equal balls. Lightly dust a plate with some of the masa, place the balls on the plate, cover with plastic wrap, and refrigerate until serving time. Reserve the rest of the masa.

To cook the crab cakes, roll them in the reserved masa to coat them evenly. Then flatten them into disks about 1 inch wide and ¾ inch thick. Heat a lightly greased or nonstick griddle or skillet over moderate to high heat. Cook the crab cakes until golden brown, about 3 minutes per side.

CORN PUREE

3   ears fresh yellow corn, husked and stringed

½   cup heavy cream

1   cup stock

1   teaspoon salt

¼   teaspoon white pepper

Grate the corn kernels from the cobs to yield 1 cup of coarse puree. In a small saucepan, combine the corn with the remaining ingredients, and cook over low heat for 10 minutes. Cool to room temperature and refrigerate, covered, until serving time.

Before cooking the Crab Cakes, gently rewarm the Corn Puree.

GARNISHES

½   recipe Red Pepper Puree (see page 112)

     Vegetable oil for deep-frying

¼   pound fresh squid ink linguine, cut into 6-inch pieces

     Fresh cilantro sprigs

Assemble the garnishes shortly before serving. Prepare the Red Pepper Puree and set it aside. In a heavy skillet or deep fryer, heat the vegetable oil to 350 degrees F on a deep-frying thermometer. Carefully scatter the pasta pieces in the oil, and fry until crisp, about 45 seconds. Drain well on paper towels and set aside.

Present the Crab Cakes with their garnishes and sauce at the table for guests to serve themselves. Or prepare individual servings: Place about 3 tablespoons of Corn Puree on each plate; drizzle about 1 tablespoon of Red Pepper Puree across the plate; place a few pieces of fried pasta across the plate; place 3 Crab Cakes in the center of the sauce; and garnish with cilantro.

GRILLED QUAIL SALAD WITH WILD MUSHROOMS AND PANCETTA LARDONS

In the modern style of salads, this main course tops a bed of mixed baby greens with hot ingredients straight from the grill and the skillet.

The only advance preparation required is marinating the quail overnight. In this presentation, the salad is served on a single platter from which guests help themselves. Alternatively, the ingredients may be arranged in similar fashion on individual plates. The salad may be eaten hot or at room temperature.

GRILLED QUAIL

6   boneless quail

1   teaspoon finely chopped fresh thyme

1   teaspoon finely chopped fresh tarragon

½   teaspoon freshly ground black pepper

1   small garlic clove, finely chopped

Begin marinating the quail the night before serving. Rub them all over with the herbs, pepper, and garlic, place them in a glass or ceramic dish, cover, and refrigerate.

Preheat the barbecue, grill, or broiler until very hot. Cook the quail close to the heat until golden brown, 2 minutes per side. Set them aside.

PANCETTA LARDONS

3   tablespoons olive oil

¼   pound pancetta, julienned

Make these just before serving the quail. Heat the olive oil in a medium skillet over moderate heat. Add the pancetta and sauté until golden brown and crisp, 2 to 3 minutes. Drain on paper towels and set aside.

WILD MUSHROOMS

3   tablespoons olive oil

2½   cups fresh wild mushrooms (chanterelles, shiitake caps, oyster mushrooms, etc.), thinly sliced

2   tablespoons white wine

2   tablespoons chicken stock

½   teaspoon kosher salt

¼   teaspoon freshly ground black pepper

¼   cup thinly sliced scallions

¼   cup diced tomato

¼   cup peeled, cored, and diced apple

Heat the oil in a medium skillet over high heat. Add the mushrooms and sauté 30 seconds. Add the wine, stock, salt, and pepper, and cook 30 seconds more. Add the scallions, cook 10 seconds more, and remove from the heat. Add the tomato and apple and toss well.

SALAD OF BABY GREENS AND JULIENNED VEGETABLES

3   cups mixed baby greens (see page 103)

½   cup julienned raw carrots, yellow bell peppers, and daikon (Japanese radish)

¼   cup Balsamic Vinaigrette (recipe on page 52)

     Salt to taste

     Freshly ground black pepper to taste

Toss the greens and vegetables with half the vinaigrette, seasoning with salt and pepper.

Spread the mushroom mixture evenly on top of a large service platter. Place the quail around the platter's perimeter. Mound the greens mixture in the center of the platter. Drizzle the remaining vinaigrette over the quail.

ASSORTED ICE CREAMS

Ice cream is the quintessential dessert for television watching. Prepare one or more of your favorite ice creams from the recipes on pages 63, 93, 136, and 145. Remove them from the freezer about 15 minutes before serving time, and present them with scoopers, bowls, and spoons so that guests can serve themselves.

APPENDIX

THROWING A SPECIAL EVENT, SOUTHERN CALIFORNIA STYLE

MANY OF THE PRECEDING MENUS MAY BE EASILY ADAPTED TO a special occasion, be it a birthday party, an anniversary, a family Easter brunch, or any number of other events. By adapting the menu and the serving style as you like or as need dictates to suit the occasion, and by doubling or tripling the recipes—or even cutting them in half—depending on how many guests you've invited, you can be assured of a stylish party featuring delicious, beautiful food.

But larger-scale events such as those regularly celebrated at the Hotel Bel-Air—weddings, gala anniversaries, bar mitzvahs, sweet-sixteen parties, and the like—require much more in the way of planning and execution to be truly successful. Following are some pointers on entertaining, Southern California–style, from the catering experts at the Hotel Bel-Air.

WHENEVER POSSIBLE, ENTERTAIN OUTDOORS

Special events at the Bel-Air traditionally take advantage of the hotel's garden setting. Most wedding ceremonies are held on the lawn beside Swan Lake with guests' chairs arranged in rows facing the gazebo, which serves either as an altar or, for Jewish weddings, the *chuppa* beneath which vows are exchanged. Tea parties are regularly staged on the hotel's terrace, making the most of the sunshine, the breezes, and the natural canopy of bougainvillea growing overhead.

If you, a family member, or a friend have a lovely and spacious garden, patio, or terrace, consider its use for your own event. And, if you have any doubt about the weather, think seriously about renting a tent. Wonderfully spacious, weatherproof tents are widely available today, complete with such amenities as lighting, heating, and even dance floors. Check your Yellow Pages for listings under the "Tents" or "Tenting" headings, or confer with a party planner.

CONSIDER THE SERVICES OF A PARTY PLANNER

Particularly for large-scale formal events, you are likely to suffer fewer headaches if you work with a professional party planner who has done this before and has all the information and contacts you will need. If you are holding the event at a hotel or other large venue specializing in parties, they will probably have professionals on-staff who can lead you step-by-step through all the necessary considerations, from choosing a photographer to finding a band, and from menu planning to seating arrangements.

But if you are throwing the party at home, or somewhere else not necessarily organized for these sort of events, ask friends for recommendations of good party planners they have worked with. Or consult your Yellow Pages under "Party Planners." Before you make your final choice, be sure to interview several different consultants, asking them how they go about organizing an event, what options they offer, and what they charge; ask them for client references, and check them out. Then select the planner who best fits your needs, and with whom you feel most comfortable.

PIN DOWN A DATE

It's impossible to place too much emphasis on this point: The farther in advance you know when the event will be, the easier you'll find it to plan everything to perfection.

For weddings, setting the date a year or more ahead is often a necessity; many professionals start booking their time that far in advance. Even simple tea parties, such as those you might throw for an anniversary or a sweet sixteen, should have their dates set several months in advance.

Weddings are often performed underneath the gazebo at the Hotel Bel-Air.

BOOK YOUR PROFESSIONALS AS SOON AS POSSIBLE

For a wedding, immediately contact your judge, minister, priest, or rabbi and confirm the date. Then, no matter what kind of event you are planning, whether with your party planner or on your own, carefully interview, select, and book all the other professionals you will need—the band leader, the photographer, the florist, and the caterer—and begin the planning process with each of them.

If at all possible, meet with each of them at the actual site chosen for the event, so they can get a feeling for the location and discuss with you any particulars related to it. Make very clear to them what your wishes and tastes are—what kind of music you like, which people absolutely must be photographed, what your favorite flowers or colors are, any special food requirements, and so on.

GO FOR THE NATURAL LOOK IN FLOWERS

Consult with your florist well in advance to discuss the options available for fulfilling the look and theme of your event, paying special attention to the many different ways in which flowers can enhance the overall effect—from altar arrangements to table displays, bouquets to boutonnieres.

The Hotel Bel-Air has evolved a particular approach to flower arranging that suits its Southern California style especially well. For the most part, floral displays are designed to look as natural as possible—almost as if the arrangement had been lifted, in its entirety, right out of the hotel's gardens.

Like the gardens, these arrangements change with the seasons, reflecting nature and the colors and moods of each particular time of year. Fresh flowers, whether grown locally or imported, combine with an abundance of foliage and other "filler"—maple leaves, snaptails, and heathers in fall; holly and pine in winter; eucalyptus, heathers, and blossoming branches such as cherry in the spring; and ivy and tropical foliage in the summer.

Judiciously used, visual surprises add an extra dimension to the Hotel Bel-Air's arrangements. Fragrant fresh herbs such as dill, rosemary, and sage sometimes join other foliage. Unusual tropical blossoms such as the spiky, spear-shaped, red-orange halaconia, and other color-ful or unusually shaped plants—African pomegranates, small artichokes on their stems, stalks of brussels sprouts, palm sheaths, and even ornamental lettuces—enhance the visual drama.

Sometimes, too, just the simplest touches have the most powerful effect. A single orchid in a plain china vase, or a low arrangement of gardenias, adds just the right touch of color and scent to a dining table without distracting from the food or from the event as a whole.

PLAN YOUR MENU WITH CARE

The Hotel Bel-Air prides itself on serving its Southern California-style cuisine at catered functions, tailoring the menu specifically to the kind of event and the time of day at which it is held.

A luncheon following a wedding, for example, will begin with hand-passed California sparkling wine and Chardonnay, and hand-passed hors-d'oeuvres; this style of service offers the guests a chance to stand and stretch their legs after the service and before the sit-down meal. Alternatively, you could set up several hors-d'oeuvres stations to which guests walk up to sample tidbits—pastas at one table, Oriental at another, Southwestern appetizers at a third, and perhaps salads, fresh fruits, cheeses, and pâtés at a fourth station. Before a dinner, you might also want to add a seafood station, and offer cocktails from a fully stocked bar.

Luncheon menus will usually include three courses: a salad or soup, a main course of fish or poultry, and a dessert. At dinner, you would probably want to include a fourth course, particularly a pasta, to precede the salad or soup. Bearing in mind that cake will probably be cut and served later on, plan on a light fruit dessert or a sorbet to be served at the end of the meal.

Ask your caterer for recommendations on the style of cake. Among the most popular wedding cakes at Hotel Bel-Air are lemon or white cake with a fresh fruit filling, or chocolate cake with raspberry filling. A basketweave design, decorated with fresh flowers adds a lively Southern California influence.

And speaking of the cake, don't serve it too soon after the meal: Guests tend to leave after the cake has been cut, and you don't want the party to end earlier than you had expected. Pass a medium-dry champagne with the cake.

Discuss all these options and questions of timing well in advance with your caterer. Make sure you also know all the details on the service staff—how many you will need and what they will cost.

It is also a common practice today in Southern California to give guests a choice of entrees—fish or poultry, for example—on their R.S.V.P. cards. (Guests who require special diets such as vegetarian, salt-free, or low-fat, will, as a rule, notify you themselves of their needs.) Then you will be able to pass all the correct numbers along to the caterer in plenty of time.

member of the catering staff or a friend of the family is assigned to receive gifts as guests arrive. The moment a gift is presented, a numbered label is stuck directly onto the package; the list-keeper asks the name of the giver, and enters it into the appropriate space on the list.

When the bridal couple or other honoree finally collects all the gifts, the numbered list accompanies them. As each numbered gift is opened, a note on its contents is entered in the space right alongside the giver's name, providing a well-organized guide for writing thank-you notes.

KEEP CLOSE TRACK OF THE GIFTS

To ensure that gifts don't go astray, the Hotel Bel-Air makes use of an ingenious but simple method that you can easily duplicate.

Before the event, sequentially numbered, pregummed labels are prepared, along with a numbered list that includes spaces beside each number for the gift-giver's name and for a desciption of the gift. A

DON'T FORGET TO HAVE FUN

With all the planning and hard work that goes into making any party successful, it's sometimes easy to forget that the point of any party is to celebrate. With all the details considered and dealt with well in advance, you should feel free, come the appointed day, to relax and enjoy your own celebration to the fullest.

KITCHEN METRICS

For cooking and baking convenience, the Metric Commission of Canada suggests the following for adapting to metric measurement. The table gives approximate, rather than exact, conversions.

SPOONS

¼ teaspoon   = 1   milliliter
½ teaspoon   = 2   milliliters
1 teaspoon   = 5   milliliters
1 tablespoon = 15 milliliters
2 tablespoons = 25 milliliters
3 tablespoons = 50 milliliters

CUPS

¼ cup = 50   milliliters
⅓ cup = 75   milliliters
½ cup = 125 milliliters
⅔ cup = 150 milliliters
¾ cup = 175 milliliters
1 cup = 250 milliliters

OVEN TEMPERATURES

200°F = 100°C
225°F = 110°C
250°F = 120°C
275°F = 140°C
300°F = 150°C
325°F = 160°C
350°F = 180°C
375°F = 190°C
400°F = 200°C
425°F = 220°C
450°F = 230°C
475°F = 240°C

INDEX

NORMAN KOLPAS would like to thank:

Dan Green, Michael Friedman, Sharon Kalman, and Bob Kosturko at Kenan Books in New York; Elaine R. Gerdau, secretary and manager of the Bel-Air Association, for the insight she offered into the history of both the hotel and the community; Phil Landon, Hotel Bel-Air concierge, and Jaime Garcia, Hotel Bel-Air for sharing their reminiscences of their long careers at the hotel.

To Katie and Jacob Kolpas, for their patience and enthusiasm throughout this project.

GEORGE MAHAFFEY would like to thank:

Hotel Bel-Air sous chefs Eamonn O'Hara, Ercolino Crugnale, and notably Tod Kawachi, whose knife skills were heavily tested; Gary Slattery who carried the ball in my absence from the kitchen; Markus Boehm, pastry chef; Scott Tucker; and Monique Slattery for her long hours testing my recipes. This endeavor was truly a team effort that relied upon the talent, skills, patience, determination, and good humor of those involved. I am proud to say thank you for your hard work and dedication.

Also, my appreciation to some people who have shown me the way in this business: Heinz Hautle, for his immense skills and modesty; Franz Buck, who opened my eyes to new ingredients and gave me the opportunity to be different and make mistakes; Peter Rosenberg, for his faith; George Morrone, for his creative spark; Roland Fasel, whose support and enthusiasm will always be remembered; and Dean Fearing for dinner at Chinois in 1989, and the guiding hand he gave me—"You Texas cats are cool!"

Finally, thank you Jamie for your patience and loving support and your clear vision. Also to my children, Michael, Tristan, Rian, and Reghan—hope you like it.

BRIAN LEATART would like to thank:

Geoff Van Dusen, photography assistant and Sally Spencer, production assistant, for their creativity and steadfast support throughout the photography.